# The Jamaican Crime Scene

# The Jamaican Crime Scene

## A Perspective

*Bernard Headley*

*Howard University Press*
*Washington, D.C.*

First published in 1994 by Eureka Press Limited, Mandeville, Jamaica

Howard University Press, Washington, D.C. 20017



Manufactured in the United States of America

This book is printed on acid-free paper.

10 9 8 7 6 5 4 3 2 1

Library of Congress Cataloging-in-Publication Data

Headley, Bernard, 1946

The Jamaican crime scene : a perspective / Bernard Headley.
p. cm.
Includes bibliographical references and index.
ISBN 0-88258-190-2 (alk. paper)
1. Crime—Jamaica. 2. Criminal justice, Administration—Jamaica.
3. Violence— Jamaica. I. Title.
HV6868.5.H43 1996
364,97292—dc20 96-5499
CIP

Cover Design: Gore Studios, Inc.

*See what Babylon a do we down here.*
*Babylon is a wicked men.*
—Rastafarian lament

*Babylon is [for the Rastafarian] the whole complex of institutions which conspire to keep the black man enslaved in the Western world and which attempt to subjugate coloured peoples throughout the world.*
—Joseph Owens, *Dread*

*If you assume that there's no hope, you guarantee that there will be no hope. If you assume that there is an instinct for freedom, there are opportunities to change things, there's a chance you may contribute to making a better world. That's your choice.*
—Noam Chomsky

For Bernie and Julian

# Contents

Foreword ........ ix

Preface and Acknowledgments ........ xiii

Prologue ........ xvii

Chapter One—A Typology ........ 1

Chapter Two—Whence Did "We" Get Such People? ........ 17

Chapter Three—A Causal Relationship Reinforced ........ 41

Chapter Four—What Is to Be Done to Achieve Greater Social Justice? ........ 43

Chapter Five—What Is to Be Done About Law Enforcement and Punishment? ........ 63

Chapter Six—Beyond the Badman Mystique ........ 89

Epilogue ........ 93

Postscript ........ 95

Notes ........ 97

Index ........ 107

## In the Ghetto*

*The stinking smell of the pit rose to the air*
*Sometimes I wonder, how comes I'm still living here*
*With garbage and filth on the road*
*Anybody would think that stinkness is our area code*

*Naked kids playing in the gully waters*
*They have nobody to think that this matters*
*As the screams of the babies break the silence*
*As we see how "mothers" exercise violence*

*Idle boys loitering in the street*
*The majority have to steal to eat*
*Pregnant teenage girls*
*They have not a friend in this world*
*The aging few who never*
*had life easy are still suffering*
*and don't know how to get out of it*

*Life is very sad in my district*
*But you should not deny that this exists*
*People: Face reality and*
*Try to change this part of society.*

*—Davene Smith*
*Kingston, Jamaica*

**Reprinted with author's permission.*

# Foreword

Since the 1970s, crime and violence have become yet another of the stereotypes harboured in the minds of those brought up on a certain perception of Jamaica. That perception sees Jamaica as a sun-drenched Caribbean isle full of the noises of calypso and reggae, laced with rum, and marked by an insatiable appetite for sex and marijuana among its 2.4 million dark-skinned inhabitants who, by habitual out-migration in the thousands, are apt to abandon what to many white tourists from the North Atlantic is the most exotic paradise on earth.

In this volume, Dr. Bernard Headley has attempted to put into perspective the reality of this textured, irritatingly complex, and admittedly sometimes "violent" isle spawned by a history of plantation slavery, protracted colonialism, and continuing economic dependency in the global dispensation, which is the reality at the end of this century.

Indeed, these states of existence at different periods of Jamaica's turbulent history have all thrived on violence itself, whether via the brutalities of enforced labour perpetrated against millions in bondage; the subjugation of political, social, and cultural rights of the vast majority under the guise of imperial protection from barbarism and savagery; or the chronic deprivation of an entire nation from self-determining participation in the operation of a world economy. That global economy, so called, continues to feed on the primary products of the developing world in return for pittance parading as fair prices but which are dictated by powerful purchasers on the world market, a market that is artfully controlled and manipulated by those very purchasers.

Such institutionalized and persistent injustice is bound to invite reactions none too civil. And when the structural devices underpinning such macro-obscenity are mirrored in "micro" form within the suffering society—as they are in a socially and economically skewed Jamaica—a resort to violence readily presents itself as one of the strategies of survival open to the dispossessed, the powerless, and the culturally denigrated. Dr. Headley draws on persuasive statistical and other empirical evidence as much as on his insights and gifts of interpretation as observer-participant to argue his position.

That position should find support among many a reader willing to take into account not only the long haul of history as a determinant of psychic formation and human behaviour but also the existential reality of social blight, which gives rhyme and reason for the phenomenon of young Jamaican men, between the ages of sixteen and twenty-four, opting for crime as the appropriate mode of what turns out to be unsafe conduct into manhood. There are no gunwomen, least of all gungirls, to speak of as emerging from the clearly anguished urban ghetto culture of contemporary Jamaica. Men, black men, may indeed be "at risk"!

Those young (black) males, one might add, are seldom able to pass their exams. They seem to like school less than their sisters or female counterparts do. But they appear to possess great reservoirs of intelligence of the sort that makes them find new form and purpose in urban America in their pursuit of criminal activities, which are frequently drug-related. They have become an awesome challenge for America's highly trained Federal Bureau of Investigation (FBI), which gives them high marks for viciousness and effectiveness even over the dreaded and ancestral Mafia.

This dubious achievement of Jamaican gangs, called "posses" (as in Hollywood Westerns), is small comfort, as Dr. Headley clearly indicates. The circumstances that spawn the posses persist in their native Jamaica with the kind of vengeance and virulence that augur ill for that other side of "paradise," which yearns for civil society, self-determination, social justice for its teeming black majority, and empowerment of all who would wish to call that island home. This hope is yet to be realized, insists Dr. Headley, who despairingly affirms the popular view that at least one dimension of Jamaica's crime and violence, that involving the use of the gun, received early support and encouragement from the leadership of the two tribes (otherwise known as political parties) hankering after power—albeit through the ballot box and with democratic fervour. The 1980 general elections—though "free" and "fair" and one of the frequent ones held since 1944—was won, and lost, via the ballot *and* the bullet. Some 800 persons lost their lives during that unforgettable campaign.

Dr. Headley is clearly disturbed by such slaughter, but he reminds the reader that Jamaica's final crime count, in any year, is likely to be well below the count per 100,000 inhabitants in the United States. The American authorities are, of course, quick on the draw with their "advisories" about unsafe travel for vacationing citizens, who form the bulk of tourist arrivals to Jamaica and other destinations in the sun-drenched, sand-filled, sea-doused Caribbean.

Whatever may be the lesson of such a statistical paradox, Dr. Headley's intention is not to score points but to find a way, a possible way, to solutions for a stubborn problem that is likely to hamper the growth and development of an otherwise vibrant and resourceful country. His scholarly analysis, besides wisely giving way to accessibility by a wider and nonacademic readership, further attempts to find some practical solutions. He actually suggests, in two chapters, "what is to be done." Humanizing Jamaica's rough-justice penal traditions and modernizing antiquated prison operations—including the much-bruited intended penal reforms—are not the least among them. He also sees an urgent need for Jamaica's planners to devise, as he puts it, "social and economic policies aimed at not merely narrowing the gap between the haves and the have-nots, but, more important, policies meant to *include and actively involve people in the ongoing process of development . . .*" [emphasis mine].

Dr. Headley must be welcomed aboard and his views heeded in what has been his people's continuing quest for a just, equitable, and civilized society—which is what independent Jamaica was, in any case, supposedly meant to be.

Rex Nettleford
Professor of Continuing Studies and Pro Vice Chancellor
University of the West Indies
Mona, Jamaica
January 1993

# Preface and Acknowledgments

Late 1992 was one of the those periods in Jamaica's post-colonial history when the nation was once again, for the umpteenth time, absorbed with its persistent bogeyman—crime. Vigorously articulating a national concern over an upsurge in violent crime were several pre-eminences in the local business establishment, among them hotel tycoon and acclaimed super patriot, Gordon "Butch" Stewart. In various speeches, interviews, and press conferences that were well covered in the Jamaican media, he commented on rising levels of "crime and disorder" and he kept pressing government to "do something" immediately.

Major portions of the October 25, 1992, edition of *The Sunday Gleaner*, including almost its entire front page, featured stories of violent crime in Jamaica, analyses of Jamaican crime, and remedies for the island's crime problem. One piece, which the paper's editorial staff seemed especially to like, was by Jamaican economist G.G. Bonnick of the World Bank. He saw Jamaica losing out on overseas investment and business opportunities because of the country's high incidence of violent crime, so he argued for "shock therapy" as the way to deal with Jamaican crime. This would involve, among other I-can't-believe-what-I'm-reading things, greater militarization of the society; liberal application of the death penalty so as to include nonhomicide and nontreason offences; placing the society under martial law while simultaneously arming every able-bodied, law-abiding citizen, thus placing them on equal footing with the "criminal"; and using South African–style "passbooks" to restrict and regulate the movement and activity of citizens.

October 1992 did, indeed, see a dramatic upsurge in violent crime. Several robberies and fatal shootings—notably in the Kingston area—were reported. The People's National Party government's most visible response was Prime Minister P.J. Patterson setting up a special task force and implementing what he called "Operation Ardent." The task force was given the responsibility "of coming up with long-term solutions to crime on the island, including the management of security."[1] And Operation Ardent gave extra powers to the security forces to crack down on crime. The leader of the opposition Jamaica Labour Party, Mr. Edward Seaga, proposed a more direct solution: the police force and the military should be "unified." This would solve two problems, Mr. Seaga said. "The police force is understaffed and under-equipped. The army is well-staffed and well-equipped. Merge these two and you will have a force that is both staffed and equipped."[2]

Well before this latest crime wave, I as a lowly "exile" Jamaican academic with a sociological curiosity about the darker doings of humankind (much so to my parents' dismay) was encouraged by then Permanent Secretary, Ministry of Public Service, Dr. Jean Marshalleck to share with a large Jamaican audience my years-long writings and analyses of Jamaican crime. I did so in a series of three rather lengthy essays, which appeared in consecutive editions of *The Sunday Gleaner* back in early 1988. The response to the series was overwhelmingly positive and gratifying, so much so that *The Gleaner*—without allowing me to update or revise them—re-ran the essays a year or so later.

The subject of crime will be with the Jamaican people for some time. They will continue to debate and dialogue over crime and violence as matters of public policy for as long as the Jamaican society is plagued with and beset by them. So what I try to do in this brief volume is simply to add, from yet another angle, to that discourse. I have revised and extended the basic themes of the earlier *Gleaner* essays and present them here as a continuous whole. My intention is to reach a broad cross section of Jamaicans (and folks interested in Jamaica), not just academics and students. Among those I especially want to reach are opinion and policy makers in- and outside the Jamaican justice system.

In addition to thanking Jean Marshalleck, I must also thank Professor Norman Girvan for his similar encouragement to "get in" on the public conversation over crime and justice in Jamaica. Furthermore, I am particularly honoured that the distinguished Rex Nettleford, after reviewing the material in manuscript form, consented to do the book's Foreword. Few others, in either academic, political, or cultural circles, really know and understand the variegated dynamics of Jamaican social life as Professor Nettleford does. My respected friend and colleague, Rory Donnelly, professor of linguistics at Northeastern Illinois University, spent much valuable time going over drafts making sure I was achieving my goals of clarity, precision, and directness of language. Fred Wellington helped me work through the mystifying wonders of computer technology; Cezley Sampson was a great facilitator; and my good friend Dudley Shields was, as he has always been, a treasured resource. I should also thank the anonymous on-the-spot reviewers who painstakingly went over the work while it was still in its manuscript stages. They gave thorough, constructive, and helpful criticisms. Along the final road to publication, editor-publisher W. Val Cambers, another astute firsthand observer of the Jamaican social and political scene, gave appreciated suggestions for improving the accuracy of the text; many thanks also go to his technical assistant Mrs. Joan Brown.

A Fulbright Senior Scholar award allowed me to spend an extended period of time in Jamaica refining conclusions presented here. It also gave me an opportunity to work with and learn from superb colleagues, and a smart group of sociology and social work students, at the University of the West Indies, Mona campus. Heartfelt appreciation to helpful staffs at the Council for the International Exchange of Scholars (Janice Byrd comes readily to mind) in Washington, D.C., and at the United States Information Agency in Kingston, Jamaica.

After all is said and done, though, I take full responsibility not only for the ideas expressed here but also for any errors of fact or judgment.

Bernard Headley
Chicago, Illinois

# Prologue

*No book is genuinely free of political bias.*
—George Orwell

*The worse place in hell is preserved for*
*those who stay neutral in times*
*of great moral crisis.*
—Dante

Few subjects evoke more alarm, more personal fear than does crime. Visitors to any major city, anywhere in the world, are told, usually by word of mouth, which sections of town to stay away from. The United States' State Department regularly warns, often using the most dire language, American tourists to avoid specific, named countries because of their crime problems.

In carrying out this little exercise, however, State Department officials seem to forget that, on American soil, some 35 million crimes were visited on the American people ages twelve years and older in 1991. Approximately 6.4 million of these victimizations consisted of violent crimes such as robbery, aggravated and simple assaults, and rape—of which some 700,000 women were victims. Another 12.5 million victimizations were crimes of theft, that is, larcenies both with and without contact between victim and offender. Add to that another 15.8 million household crimes.[1]

Furthermore, America is currently in the midst of a gun crisis that can no longer be considered just a manifestation of its "pioneer spirit." Rather, it has become a "costly global embarrassment," as author Erik Larson put it.[2] That a gun-crimes crisis exists in America should be well beyond dispute by now, given the bleak statistics on gunshot death and damage.

Between 1990 and 1992, firearms killed 60,000 Americans, more than the number of U.S. soldiers killed in the Vietnam war. On average, handguns account for 22,000 American deaths a year. Well before the infamous Los Angeles rebellion, in spring 1991, which ensued in the wake of not-guilty verdicts of four white police officers accused of beating nearly to death black motorist Rodney King,[3] the guns of Los Angeles County alone killed or wounded 8,050—several times over the number of U.S. casualties in the Persian Gulf War, according to a survey by the *Los Angeles Times*.[4] In early 1993, the Federal Centers for Disease Control and Prevention (CDC) released a study showing that 4,173 teenagers in the United States died from gunshot wounds in 1990. The toll for ages fifteen through nineteen was the highest in the world.[5] As a follow-up to the CDC study, in April 1993, the *Chicago Tribune* ran a special series of articles on gun violence in Chicago's inner city, declaring in that series that gunshot killings are now an everyday fact of life for many American children. Fourteen Chicago children (ages twelve and younger) who lived on the city's black sides were slain by gunfire within the first three months of 1993. "Death is not an abstraction for many Chicago-area children," wrote the series author, "but a grim ritual almost as commonplace as going to the movies. A dark culture has woven its way into their minds, games and dreams, and dimmed their view of the world."[6]

Still, handguns terrorize far more Americans than they actually kill. Recently released Department of Justice statistics show that, in America, every twenty-four hours handgun-wielding assailants rape thirty-three women, rob 575 people, and assault another 1,116.[7]

Visitors to the United States have hardly been unaffected by American crime and violence. In October 1992, a teenage Japanese exchange student, who came to the States to study American culture, was shot and killed by a Baton Rouge, Louisiana, homeowner. The youngster had mistakenly wandered on to the man's property while in search of another address—a home where a Halloween party was being given. In April 1993, in Miami, Florida, a German tourist who got lost in her rental car after leaving the Miami International Airport was robbed, savagely beaten, and run over in front of her mother and two young children. She became the sixth tourist slain in Florida between December 1992 and April 1993.[8] One week following the Miami killing, a Scottish visitor was also robbed and brutally murdered in New Orleans' French Quarter.

With incidents like these in mind, plus their knowledge of the United States' broader crime trends, little wonder that the Japanese authorities, in perhaps a not-altogether-friendly gesture of one-up-manship, saw fit not so long ago to include the United States on their list of "World's Most Dangerous Places" to visit. The authorities at the U.S. State Department were not amused.

Explaining crime, whether violent or property, whether in the prosperous United States or in poor "little" Jamaica, is, however, no easy task. In fact, few other topics are more subject to varying points of view and different "theories" than is crime. The proverbial man-in-the-street opinion is that crime is a peculiar type of errant behaviour found only among individuals from a certain social and otherwise distinctly defined segment of society. Criminal acts are, therefore, attributable to wicked, evil, and utterly irredeemable persons from the "dregs" of the social order. Criminals are people, if you can call them that, whom civilized society should lock away, if not permanently banish—or kill.

Amazingly, the view of crime as peculiar behaviour trait, or "predisposition," is not strikingly different from some of the still widely accepted views in respected academic circles, where more than a few influential social thinkers see crime as a function of "human nature."[9]

To local, regional, national, and international law-enforcement agencies, especially the more sophisticated ones, crime is a matter of "logistics," a management problem that experts trained in "the law," the methods of investigative police science, modes of incarceration, and the effective use of force can, if given sufficient resources, handle. Thus, in Jamaica, as in the United States, from the late 1960s to the present, the repressive model of crime control, previously articulated in half-hearted ways, has been fully realized. That model consists of maximum security institutions housing large numbers of prisoners; military-staged and, often enough (as in Jamaica), military-directed policing; enhanced firepower; proliferation of private security systems; and legislative support at the national level for increased criminalization, punitive sentencing, and capital punishment.

This volume takes quite a different view from the one that sees crime as primarily a problem of individual choice or as the result of some latent predisposition. Nor do I view the solution to crime as lying mostly in the application of "efficient," "scientific," or massive law enforcement. "Street" or "conventional" crimes result mainly from particular kinds of social and economic arrangements, I argue, and they are not management problems that can be ameliorated and ultimately solved merely by applying state-of-the-art high technology or managerial problem-solving, criminal-justice approaches.

But such an understanding of crime is, one might challenge, ideological. I concede the charge. Let us be clear, however, on what we mean by an ideologically, or politically, grounded understanding. Simply put, ideology suggests an implicit system of values and beliefs that defines right and wrong, a preference for a specific line of thinking, an attachment to a certain world view or way of looking at things—or, as the philosopher Max Scheler put it, one's "natural way of looking at the world."[10] Above all else, an ideology represents a commitment to work, through use of political processes, for change. An ideology is really nothing more and nothing less than just this, the ponderous, heavy-handed writings of Karl Marx notwithstanding. So, really, it is quite silly to talk about "the end of ideology," because as long as there are people there will always be competing belief systems and different ways of viewing and interpreting the universe. My task here, then, is to convince the reader, through thoughtful reasoning and persuasive analysis of information that everyone has access to, of the soundness of my position. But I also believe that a more fundamental, moral issue is at stake, i.e., whose ideology will govern a political order? So when discussing how in a politically ordered society to control or reduce crime, for me the bedrock values question is this: is an ideology of brute force, retribution, and perpetual social *in*justice for those at the bottom of society the best way to deal with a nation's crime problem? Or, shouldn't we be contemplating an ideology of social and economic justice and a justice system that repairs and rehabilitates in the interest of a common good?

The discourse here clearly leans toward the latter. I present my own non–value-free analysis (or view, as some might call it) of the dynamics of crime and justice in Jamaica. I try to give a multidimensional but always structurally based presentation of crime and violence in the society *itself* and of the internal causes behind the export—primarily to the United States—of Jamaican crime.

Although I agree that some types of crime do result from pre-existing webs of confusion in some individuals' minds, and concede that guilty persons should "pay" for their crime(s), I also maintain that external forces beyond emotional and mental impairment push or "drive" many Jamaicans into committing the kinds of misdeeds we are here calling "street" crimes. They are forces that transcend simplistic, one-dimensional notions of choice or human failings. Instead, they have specific political, economic, and historical roots that manifest themselves in the social and political disabilities of race *and* class, all of which are further compounded by the workings of a dubious justice system. The policies of "law and order" are, I maintain, simplistic and reductionist. They ignore the complex economic, social, political, and ideological nature of crime.

I conclude that only if Jamaicans everywhere move toward reconstructing a society for the common good—one based on peace, social and economic justice, and respect—can they hope to have a society with less, not more, crime. Am I then talking about going back to some idealized notion of socialism as *the* way for reducing or eliminating crime? No and yes. One would be foolish not to admit that, indeed, several things went wrong with the practice of Soviet and East European socialism; and that, at this historical moment, several things are *still wrong* with, say, Cuban and Chinese socialism. The specific issues attendant to those specific cases are, of course, beyond the scope of this collection.[11]

Consider, for a moment, however, the larger theoretical point. Norman Girvan makes the persuasive argument that the popular-based socialist movements of the recent past did not exactly solve the developing countries' problem of economic backwardness and dependency, even where allowed a measure of institutional/governmental autonomy. "After nearly fifty years of attempts at state-sponsored social engineering informed by social science, the problem of world poverty is much more massive and seemingly more intractable than before," he argues. "It is my central belief," he continues, "that this underlies the fact that in the

1980s, confidence in the social sciences [was] replaced by a rehabilitation of the 'magic of the marketplace'. . . ."[12]

His timely retrospection notwithstanding, Professor Girvan would, I suspect, still agree that all the socialist projects that were attempted in Eastern Europe, Latin America, and parts of Africa—including those that "failed"—did move whole societies beyond the ugly spectre of routinized street crime. As if to prove the point, now in the aftermath of the fall of communism, many of the former communist states of Eastern Europe are experiencing an unprecedented rise in levels of street crime. Czech Republic (formerly one-half of Czechoslovakia) authorities, for example, complain of a dramatic increase in prostitution—and some of the crimes associated with it, including robbery and murder—as the "price of freedom."[13]

The idea that an unencumbered "free" marketplace (i.e., an environment where government has no real role to play in tackling economic problems) can eradicate the forces that most clear-thinking people agree cause crime is, I maintain, a false ideology. If a society, any society, is ever to move beyond social and economic backwardness, government has to assume responsibility for matters falling outside the usual national defence and "security" concerns. In the global economy that characterizes the present epoch, government will also have to exert influence on the society's educational, training, information, communication, and transportation systems (its infrastructure); protect the environment; set priorities for research and technology development; and flex its muscles in areas of economic cooperation, trade, investment, and capital inflows.

And only government can set policy, make laws, and foster the kind of national and social cohesion that will mitigate against the forces that invariably cause crime—pervasive social and economic inequality, racial marginalization, permanent joblessness, lack of access to legitimate opportunity, and ghettoization, among others.

My ideas and analyses of the causes of Jamaican street crime are not new. In fact, the basic themes are as old as Christendom. They posit that social justice must *a priori* precede expectations for social peace or "public safety." These themes are equally correct today, I maintain, as they were five, six, or even a hundred years ago.

I challenge here some of the more conventional "solutions" and "remedies" now being put forth for Jamaica's crime problem. As in times past, the Jamaican people are again hearing a greater call to arms for more of the same old tried and *failed* solutions, with, perhaps, greater intensification in their implementation—as with the officially heralded Anti-Crime Investigation Detachment, which carries the disturbing acronym ACID. Often missed is that not only has the patient been unaffected by the medication we have been force-feeding her, but also she is having a bad reaction to it and is in effect dying from it. Rather than taking a method, trying it, and if it fails, admitting defeat and trying another, some of the nation's leading lights and government leaders are insisting that we ought to double the dosage.

Jamaica's own "rich and famous," influential hotelier Gordon "Butch" Stewart, calls, for instance, for Jamaican law enforcement to receive "help" from the American, British, or Israeli security forces in combatting crime in Jamaica. What he and others, such as Jamaica Labour Party leader Edward Seaga, are calling for is more law enforcement and more punishment. Never mind that the nation's prisons and jails are filled beyond normal human capacity, bringing down more disgrace and international embarrassment on a supposedly humane and civilized people. Also not generally realized is that the Jamaican security forces are responding rather well (i.e., in the traditional ways) to crime.

In fact, if we are to believe official reports, the Jamaican police typically outshine their American and British big-city counterparts in the rates at which they solve, or at least "clear up" by arrest, crime incidents. Reported "cleared up" rates in excess of 60 percent (as reported for 1991) for *all* serious crimes are not unknown to the Jamaican police. Contrast that with rates for most large U.S. cities, such as New York, Los Angeles, and Chicago, whose law-enforcement agencies showed, for 1990, clearance rates of less than 25 percent for all serious or "Crime Index" offences brought to their attention.[14] Similarly, in 1992, London's bobbies (whose city has in recent years been experiencing an upsurge in violent crime) were successful in clearing up a mere 29 percent of all reported crimes, according to a March 1993 American National Public Radio (NPR) story.[15] Furthermore, the Jamaican police often are known to react to crime in the extra-legal, expeditious ways that many in the society expect, and have indeed asked, them to: that is, to bust heads and bring in the "criminals" more dead than alive. In all too many instances, if reports from acclaimed international human rights organizations such as Americas Watch are true, these expeditious ways of enforcing the law in Jamaica would make the Los Angeles cop beating of Rodney King look like a Sunday-evening soccer skirmish.[16]

So long as our emphasis and discourse on crime remain strictly along lines of control and official brutality rather than prevention, on punishment rather than redemption and rehabilitation, we will continue to have a society that is plagued and beset by crime. A society that offers little or no hope to the masses of its people and seeks only to further destroy rather than humanize and redeem its children is a society that will forever reap the whirlwind of more crime. We need, therefore, new and imaginative ways of thinking about crime and violence prevention, since the causes, as we should well know by this time, are embedded in a social system of deprivation and neglect, and a society which itself practices and condones acts of official violence—for example, its enthusiastic support of the death penalty, among other gloomy things.

For a society *not* to experience consistently high levels of street crime, policy makers will have to seek ways to build into the social fabric support strategies—including a wide-ranging, effective training and educational system—that are deliberately designed to intervene into the lives of troubled and/or "crime-prone" youngsters. "Tougher" law enforcement *by itself* will never seriously reduce crime; it only displaces and perhaps delays its occurrence. As far as "the law" goes, we should be thinking, instead, of new and more creative ways in which it, and more specifically law enforcement, can be transformed into agencies of a different sort—how, for example, they may exert a more proactive and less reactive front-line influence against crime. Finally, we need to think through ways that the larger Jamaican society can resurrect, rehabilitate, and reconstruct lives that have been distorted and deformed by their resort to crime.

So if Mr. Stewart and others in the Jamaican business establishment want to play larger roles than merely being trumpeters at the potentially crumbling Jericho walls, and if they want continued secure access to North American tourist dollars, I would urge them to put a small fraction of their enormous resources into some of the crime prevention and rehabilitation strategies I discuss here. Enlightened self-interest and a presumed desire for a better society require no less of them. The Jamaican people do not need, in the final analysis, any Israeli Mossad, American FBI or CIA, or British MI5 to come in and solve for them their crime problem. All it takes is a sensible, humane, and caring people deciding what kind of society they want to have.

Now some specifics on the chapters and organization of this book.

In chapter one, I attempt to separate out the kinds of predatory crime that now plague the Jamaican society, and which are the more serious to its development, from other types of crime that have less long-term structural consequences. In chapter two, I contend that how Jamaica got all its "bad" criminal "elements" is no mystery—not those criminals we have kept at home or those we somehow managed to ship abroad, only to have them later ejected from distant ports and returned to Jamaica. We got them all, I argue, from the particular historical contradictions of Jamaica's social and economic system and from the vagaries of the country's national political culture.

Chapter three is a friendly review of an excellent empirical study that reinforces my basic proposition that much Jamaican crime is the result of too many people being denied the fruits, the rewards, of the nation's independence, limited though they might be.

Having outlined the causes and nature of Jamaica's crime problem, I offer in chapters four and five some carefully thought-through recommendations. I present them, presumptuously I admit, as a series of "What is to be done" (the phrase is Lenin's) recommendations. I deliberately try here to blend what I perceive as the Jamaican social reality of crime with my own lived and research experience as a sociologist/criminologist in the United States. I try to translate my ideas about equality and a critical pedagogy into what Stuart Hall calls "the language of experience, moral imperative, and common sense, thus providing a 'philosophy' in the broader sense."[17]

Attempting to meld an American experience and understanding of crime and justice into a practical perspective on the Jamaican crime scene is not all that far-fetched. Some basic commonalties in regard to root causes and a certain race-class trajectory are indeed present for both the American and Jamaican societies. Moreover, several important lessons can be learned from a bankrupt American policy of more law and order and of building more prisons. Among other things, we learn that, where given official (not just popular) support, a variety of community outreach projects and implementation of progressive models of law enforcement and punishment *do* reduce crime. Nothing but good things would follow if aspects of these newer, more realistic trends were adapted—or even borrowed wholesale—for Jamaica. In the same way that the Jamaican security forces are being encouraged to acquire, from the Americans, weaponry training and high-tech means for "catching" criminals—something they've in fact been doing for some time now—so, too, can the larger Jamaican society benefit from the Americans in their attempts at dealing in creative and imaginative ways with the problem of crime, half-hearted and feeble as these attempts most times are.

With this in mind, chapter four specifically focuses on the kinds of deliberate social and economic policies the Jamaican people might institute to reduce levels of crime. A narrowing of the gap between the haves and the have-nots is a must, but equally important is finding ways to involve all Jamaicans more actively in the ongoing process of development. I also discuss a few practical and immediately implementable strategies for constructively engaging youths who might otherwise drift into crime.

Chapter five examines ways in which we might reform how we enforce the law and mete out punishment. Here, again, I urge an approach of involving the society at large, because, like it or not, crime is the entire nation's problem. As such, ideas as to how we dispense justice should always be molded within the arena of public discourse. Never in a civilized, democratic society should secret official plans be hatched up—*a la* the now-long-forgotten Green Bay, St. Catherine, killings of a bunch of youthful suspects in the late 1970s by the island's security forces—as to what some limited "we" are going to do about offenders who, agreed, are "no angels," as one then-prominent government minister allegedly said of the Green Bay victims.

Finally, chapter six looks at some of the deeper cultural forces that have underpinned and nurtured the myth, and the aura, of Jamaica's most feared thugs and badmen. This chapter ends on one additional optimistic note: the time may be right for broadening—and deepening—a communitarian ethos in Jamaica, one that, more than all the various interventionist strategies we might propose, would serve as *the* lasting bulwark against crime.

# 1
# A Typology

*Dis one have a gun*
*Dat one have a gun*
*An' when it pop*
*Another one drop.*
—Peter Tosh, "Peace Treaty"

It's a cold Saturday night in January. A group of revellers, a microcosm of the Jamaican working class, which had to go abroad in order to find work, are celebrating in typical yard style the end of the work week in Chicago.

They are doing so in one of the new reggae hot spots that have been springing up like wild orchids amid the interstices of the "concrete jungles" of Chicago's North Side. Between the live, on-stage performances of a local band, the party people are jamming to the recorded *soca* music of "Black Stallion," "Arrow," "Calypso Rose." (The period was just slightly pre-dancehall.) They mellow out to the sounds of Dennis Brown and the "cool ruler," Gregory Isaacs. "Cool down de pace," pleads the irrepressible Isaacs.

The crowd revs up again to full-length platters by deejay "King Yellowman," whose lyrics engage the dancers in an execration of a woman's body parts.

Over by the bar, some of the older men, now properly juiced on Jamaican rum and Red Stripe Beer, are engrossed in a rambling discussion on Jamaican politics. Talk, like liquor, is cheap.

A group of younger men dressed in the styles and fashion of their hip-hop generation saunters in from off the bustling sidewalk. A couple of them begin a friendly banter over the price of admission with the woman cloistered behind the bullet-proof Plexiglass enclosure at the entranceway. They pay it and then enter the hall with a slow, deliberate gait, as they proceed to "check out" the stock of available *dawtas.* Across the dance floor, heads, shoulders, arms, and waists are gyrating in a steady, rhythmic, pulsating roll. In stark contrast to the shivering, sub-zero temperature outside, the room is hot, steamy. *Dis a seshaan, mahn!*

Then sometime between midnight and the wee hours of the breaking new day—about the time that local ordinances require that all liquor sales cease—the air is pierced by the deafening sound of what to the untrained ear seems like an earth-shattering distortion coming from one of the giant speakers which had been pumping out steady streams of thousand-odd-watt music all night long. But when the noise repeats itself in quick, rapid-fire bursts, the music uninterrupted, the revellers realize that this is no stereophonic distortion: this is the sound of gunfire! The laughter and the gaiety that only a few moments before had filled the room is replaced by the shrieks of frightened men and women, punctured by cries of "Lawd Jesus Chris'!"

Everyone runs for cover. The tune "Every Posse Get Flat" now suddenly takes on the literal, deadly meaning for which it must have been intended. The bartender cowers beneath the bar; one diminutive man dives into a free-standing trash can; the sound man, who only hours before had exercised extreme care in setting up all that gadgetry lest they be harmed in the slightest way, now uses those same gadgets to barricade himself. The carnival comes to an abrupt stop.

From their flattened positions and with both hands pressed against the backs of their heads, the petrified patrons begin cautiously, slowly, to peer into the center of the darkened room as they try to comprehend what on earth had "hit" them. Standing there are two of Jamaica's "children of Sisyphus" (to borrow Orlando Patterson's term[1]): a couple of uprooted, unrighteous toughs dressed in tams and designer-labelled warm-up outfits, their heavily tinted sunglasses menacingly set against the din and smoke coming from hastily discarded cigarettes. Around their necks hang half of Africa's gold reserve. Their itchy fingers are nervously coiled around the trigger mechanisms of two manifestations of civilization's most awesome solution for the Malthusian problem of too many people. Using nine-millimetre converted Uzi submachine guns, the youths had just mowed down, at point blank range, one of the male revellers, whose chest is torn apart by rounds of hollowpoint bullets. Another lies seriously injured in a nearby corner; blood oozes from his riddled body like water gushing from a broken standpipe. The scene is straight out of Dodge City.

The gunmen, in typical cowboy style, had busted their way into the hall. They had an argument to "settle" with their victims. That argument—over either drug turf or drug money—was now settled, at least with one, in the most decisive way. Their mission of waste and destruction accomplished, the marauders, still clutching the smoking instruments of death with firm, sinewy hands, stealthily back away from the carnage and out through the swinging doors. They speed off into the winter night in a shiny, new, vanity-plated silver "Beemer"—as in BMW.

The incident did actually happen in Chicago. But it's the kind of incident that has been occurring with alarming regularity in several North American cities, giving, since about the mid-1980s, newfound negative prominence to Jamaicans living in the United States. Witness below some of 1980s' news stories that appeared in several prominent American dailies about Jamaicans in the United States being involved in drug- and gang-related crimes:

- *Oakland, N.J., August 5, 1985.* Two women who were caught in a crossfire at a picnic here Sunday, which left 2 dead and 19 injured, today linked the gun battle to longstanding feuds over Jamaican politics. Of the 19 hurt, 9 were wounded, while 10 were injured in the panic set off by the shootings. . . . The Bergen County Prosecutor, Larry McClure, said at a news conference today that investigators had not yet determined what led to the shootout that witnesses said went on for 10 minutes amid a throng of 2,000 people. Among the theories they are pursuing, he said, is that the shootings stemmed from political disputes, drug deals, gang warfare or other personal feuds.[2]
- *Los Angeles, Calif., October 21, 1987.* A crackdown on criminal gangs from Jamaica resulted in 124 arrests, including five in Southern California. Stephen E. Higgins, director of the Bureau of Alcohol, Tobacco, and Firearms, said in Washington that the raids took place over two days in 13 states and the District of Columbia. Los Angeles-based Immigration and Naturalization Service agents arrested five Jamaicans in Inglewood and seized a small quantity of illegal drugs, said Mike Flynn, a senior special agent. Flynn said that Jamaican drug traffickers are among the most violent, and may be the source of 60 percent of the crack cocaine supply in the United States.[3]
- *New York, N.Y., August 8, 1985.* The Customs Service seized an Air Jamaica jetliner at Kennedy International Airport yesterday, saying the line had failed to provide adequate security against narcotics smuggling. . . . The seizure occurred as the plane was about to take off for Kingston with 245 people. Mr. Michael Kaufman (a Customs spokesman) said he thought it was the first seizure of a commercial plane at an airport in the New York area under a Federal Law that enables confiscating vehicles suspected of transporting narcotics. . . . Since last October, Customs has seized almost 10,000 pounds of marijuana arriving on Air Jamaica flights—mostly in baggage not checked on the planes' manifests, according to Mr. Kaufman.[4]
- *Waukegan, Ill., March 9, 1987.* Valentine Reid, charged in connection with last week's "Jamaican Get-Together" shootout in the hall of St. Nikolas Serbian Orthodox Church, walked out of Victory Memorial Hospital Sunday. Reid was being held in lieu of $500,000 bond at the hospital, where he was recovering from a gunshot wound to the left thigh. . . . Earlier Waukegan Detective Bureau personnel had become the answering service for calls being recorded on a beeper confiscated from Reid after the shooting incident. The calls were from people apparently wanting to make drug purchases.[5]

Indeed, since the mid-1980s the criminal acts of a few have turned the attention of the American criminal justice authorities toward *all* Jamaicans living in the United States. Jamaicans have by and large been depicted as a people with a "different conception of life," to coin U.S. (Army) General William Westmoreland's infamous characterization of the Vietnamese. Assisted in large measure by the popular media (including Hollywood movie depictions), the image of the Jamaican that is often presented is that of a violent, gun-toting, doped-up, dreadlocked, savage black male who trafficks in illegal drugs.

We dare not disclaim Jamaican involvement in the American narcotics market.[6] Federal officials believe that, since 1984, a large number of overseas Jamaicans (primarily in Canada, the United States, and Great Britain) have created a widespread criminal organization made up of several gangs. These gangs have been involved primarily in importing and distributing illegal drugs.[7] By the end of the 1980s, the gangs, which call themselves "posses," were said to have over 5,000 members and associates. The period's reigning gangs included the Spanglar Posse, the Dog Posse, the Tel Aviv Posse, the Water House Posse, the Banton Posse, the Dunkirk Posse, and the Shower Posse—names derived from Grade "B" American Westerns and from specific areas of the Kingston ghetto where some of them originated. "Today, gangs such as the Jamaican posses are all more violent or much wealthier than La Cosa Nostra" (also known as the Mafia), says an April 1992 *Newsweek* article.[8]

The activities of the Jamaican posses were first investigated by Interpol, which was looking for links between gangs and vast quantities of guns that were being smuggled into Jamaica. The U.S. Bureau of Alcohol, Tobacco, and Firearms (ATF) first became aware of the posses in 1984, when Interpol asked for American law-enforcement assistance in tracing several firearms that had been recovered in Jamaica. The ATF-Interpol investigation traced the gun route to the Shower Posse, a West Kingston–based gang.[9] At one time the posses controlled all crack and street-level gun-running operations in the New York, Washington, D.C., Philadelphia, Miami, Fort Lauderdale, Kansas City, Houston, and Dallas metropolitan areas. Their members' seeming reflexive tendency toward use of extreme violence was never underestimated. "They are shooters. They'll shoot cops, they'll shoot each other, and they'll shoot innocent bystanders. They scare the hell out of us," one ATF official said of the posses, in 1987.[10]

Between 1987 and 1988 some 300 to 400 homicides committed in the United States were attributed to the Jamaican posses. A January 1988 report in *U.S. News & World Report* on the broader problem of the resurgence, in the 1980s, of "ethnic gangs" in America stated: "Police and prosecutors are puzzled, and in some cases awe-struck, by the sophistication of the Asian gangs, but they are positively alarmed at the propensity for violence of Jamaican criminals."[11]

## The Problem Begins at Home

I contend here that acts of criminal violence perpetrated by Jamaicans living in the United States are direct spill-overs from high levels of crime and violence in the Jamaican society itself. So whether it's a carnage at a "session" on Chicago's North Side, a drive-by shooting in Washington, D.C., a for-hire killing in Miami, or a shootout in a New Jersey state park, none can be dismissed as an aberration or as simply the isolated, violent predisposition of a desperate few. Rising levels of crime and violence, even though committed by only a minority within the overseas Jamaican community, are inevitable by-products, I submit, of the society Jamaicans have built in the home country.

Creeping levels of crime and violence have, in fact, been Jamaica's lot since about the late 1960s. Much of the society's deep-rooted social-structural problems (discussed in depth in the next chapter) began to bubble over just about then. Later, in the 1980s, violent crime jumped to unprecedented levels. A spot check of the island's leading newspaper, *The Daily Gleaner*, revealed a host of attention-grabbing crime stories, all having occurred over a six-day period during summer 1984. They appeared under headlines such as the following:

- "Gunmen Kill Three in St. Catherine: M16s Used,"
- "Gunmen Kill One in St. Elizabeth,"
- "Householder Shot, Gunmen Leave Gun,"
- "Inspector of Police Slain,"
- "Murder Witness, Daughter Slain: 50 Held in Giant Manhunt,"
- "East Kingston Guns Silenced But. . .,"
- "Gunmen Killed in Shootout,"
- "Police Kill Five in Shootouts."

The brutal murder—or execution, as has been alleged—of reggae superstar Peter Tosh, in September 1987, was only one of several slayings that occurred in this period.[12]

A number of studies on violent crime trends in Jamaica arrive at one general conclusion: actual rates of street-level violence skyrocketed in the years following the granting of political independence from Great Britain, in 1962. Dudley Allen, for example, notes that violent crime rates doubled over the period 1962 to 1975,[13] and William Wilbanks observes that, over the same period, manslaughter rates increased by 167 percent, robbery by 771 percent, rape by 160 percent, felonious wounding by 137 percent, and shooting with intent by 1,350 percent.[14]

Inherent to the Jamaica crime data are, of course, numerous measurement and reliability problems—as is true for crime data for any number of countries, developing and developed.[15] Be that as it may, table 1 shows a national pattern of relatively stable, and low, figures for number of reported violent crimes for the early 1960s.

TABLE 1. Number of reported violent offences for selected two-year periods, 1961–1992. (NA denotes not available.)

| Years | Homicide | Man-slaughter | Felonious wounding | Robbery | Rape |
|---|---|---|---|---|---|
| 1961–62 | 183 | 144 | 466 | NA | NA |
| 1963–64 | 219 | 110 | 516 | NA | NA |
| 1965–66 | 228 | 119 | 898 | NA | NA |
| 1968–69 | 130 | 85 | NA | NA | 352 |
| 1971–72 | 297 | 125 | NA | NA | 544 |
| 1973–74 | 439 | 150 | NA | NA | 692 |
| 1976–77 | 776 | 96 | NA | 6,406 | 1,501 |
| 1979–80 | 1,299 | 60 | NA | NA | NA |
| 1982–83 | 829 | 85 | NA | 7,607 | 1,718 |
| 1987–88 | 856 | 87 | 1,706 | 9,336 | 2,125 |
| 1989–90 | 981 | 85 | 1,326 | 9,862 | 2,096 |
| 1991–92 | 1,119 | 58[a] | 560[a] | 4,987[a] | 1,687 |

[a]Figures are for 1991 only.

Sources: Lacey[16]; *Statistical Abstract*, 1972, 1975, 1981; *Economic and Social Survey*, 1983, 1991; *Statistical Yearbook of Jamaica*, 1978, 1981, 1990; *The Sunday Gleaner*, October 25, 1992; *The Sunday Gleaner*, January 3, 1993.

In the 1970s and through most of the 1980s, these numbers rose dramatically. For the years 1961 and 1962, for example, the number of reported homicides was 183; fifteen years later, in 1976 and 1977, 776 killings were reported, for an increase of some 324 percent. Four-hundred and sixty-six felonious woundings were reported for 1961 and 1962; in 1987 and 1988 the number shot up to 1,706, an increase of 266 percent. This pattern is true also for rape, where the increase in number of reported rapes for the years 1987 and 1988 (2,125) was over 500 percent greater than the number reported for 1968 and 1969. Number of homicides (or murder in the official designation) leapfrogged even more dramatically in the years 1979 and 1980 over the immediately preceding years, then decreased almost as dramatically in the years immediately following. The reason for this sudden jump in the combined total for 1979 and 1980 is that 1980 was a particularly violent election year, the most violent, in fact, in the country's postindependence political history. The police attributed a significant number of the island's close to 900 killings in 1980—the highest ever for a single year—to the high level of political violence associated with the October 1980 general election. (I will discuss the roots of Jamaican political violence in chapter two.)

Unlike most other countries where number of property crimes usually exceed the number of violent crimes, in Jamaica, at least during the decade of the 1980s up through the early 1990s, the number of reported violent crimes consistently outnumbered the number of reported property crimes (table 2). The total number of violent crimes reported in one year, 1988, for example, was 19,456, whereas the total number of reported non–drug-related property crimes (burglary, larceny, and so forth) was 15,336, smaller by some 20 percent than the number of violent crimes. The same general pattern held for 1989, 1990, and 1991.

Illegal drug trafficking (what the authorities refer to as "breaches of the dangerous drug law"), exclusive of all other crimes, shows an unexpected pattern. The predictable trend of annual increases in these crimes is true here as for all other serious crimes, particularly so in the mid-1970s through late 1980s. Thus, for example, table 3 shows that in the years 1966 through 1968 the local police investigated just over 3,100 cases of drug trafficking. Fourteen years later, in a similar three-year period, 1982 through 1984, the number skyrocketed to over 13,000. Toward the end of the 1980s, however, the numbers show an unexpected decline. For example, the number of cases for 1988 through 1990 dropped a significant 14.3 percent from the previous two-year period.

We can attribute this unexpected decline to three possibly alternating reasons. First, crackdown by the Jamaican authorities—which included, among other things, use of what some billed as police "terror squads" and threats to shoot out of the sky suspected drug-smuggling aircraft—could have indeed produced a widely hoped-for deterrent effect. Second, because of the high political stakes Washington, D.C., had placed on Jamaica and other Caribbean/Latin American political authorities to succeed in the war against the international flow of illegal drugs, it is

TABLE 2. Number of reported property crimes versus total reported violent crimes, 1987–1991

| Offence | 1987 | 1988 | 1989 | 1990 | 1991 |
|---|---|---|---|---|---|
| Burglary | 2,102 | 1,839 | 1,811 | 1,961 | 1,846 |
| House break-in | 2,868 | 2,584 | 2,687 | 2,973 | 3,011 |
| Other break-ins | 2,922 | 2,831 | 2,851 | 3,011 | 3,220 |
| Larceny/person | 1,417 | 1,297 | 1,101 | 1,069 | 1,130 |
| Larceny/dwelling | 736 | 686 | 630 | 770 | 784 |
| Praedial larceny | 597 | 435 | 498 | 450 | 544 |
| Larceny of motor vehicle | 497 | 361 | 377 | 385 | 582 |
| Larceny from motor vehicle | 457 | 344 | 338 | 297 | 357 |
| Others | 5,556 | 4,959 | 4,891 | 5,242 | 5,002 |
| Total property crimes | 17,152 | 15,336 | 15,184 | 16,158 | 16,476 |
| Total violent crimes | 20,647 | 19,456 | 19,886 | 20,698 | 18,522 |

Source: *Economic and Social Survey*, 1991.

TABLE 3. Number of police investigations for cases of narcotics trafficking for selected years

| Years | Cases | Percent change |
|---|---|---|
| 1966–68 | 3,117 | — |
| 1969–71 | 5,576 | +78.0 |
| 1972–74 | 8,963 | +60.0 |
| 1975–77 | 11,679 | +30.3 |
| 1978–80 | 12,171 | +4.2 |
| 1982–84 | 13,350 | +9.6 |
| 1985–87 | 12,989 | −2.7 |
| 1988–90 | 11,119 | −14.3 |

Sources: *Statistical Yearbook of Jamaica*, 1978, 1981, 1991.

altogether likely that the figures reported here could have been "adjusted" downward to leave the impression of increased local police efficiency. The third possibility is that during this period most of the drug action was taking place *not* in Jamaica but overseas—primarily on the streets of urban "Amerika," to which significant numbers of career Jamaican offenders were at the time migrating.

Even more interesting than the anomaly as regards the illegal drug figures is that, despite the troubling number of reported violent crime, actual crime *rates*, as a ratio of crime to population,[17] for all major or serious non–drug-related crimes *declined* in the period 1980 through 1989. Table 4 gives rates per 100,000 population for all reported serious crime—violent and property—for selected years between 1980 and 1990. In 1980, with a total population of approximately two million people, the country's overall crime rate (i.e., for all offences) stood at 2,580 offences per 100,000 population, a figure which was among the highest in the English-speaking Caribbean. That figure, however, was still way below the U.S. overall rate of 5,900 per 100,000 population for that same year,[18] despite 1980 being an abnormally high violent crime year for Jamaica.

In 1988, the rate for all offences in Jamaica seemed to bottom out at 1,740 offences per 100,000 population. It began ratcheting up again in 1989, however, and stood at 2,050 at the last available count (i.e., in 1991). Both Jamaica's 1988 and 1991 overall rates per 100,000 population were, again, significantly below the U.S. rates of 5,741 and 5,897 for those identical years, according to the U.S. Department of Justice's *Uniform Crime Reports*.

I attribute a substantial portion of the 1981 through 1988 declines in the Jamaican crime rate to a spurt in the size of the nation's total

TABLE 4. Rate per 100,000 population for all serious non–drug-related crimes for selected years

| Year | Rate |
|---|---|
| 1980 | 2,580.0 |
| 1981 | 2,466.0 |
| 1982 | 2,455.0 |
| 1983 | 2,399.0 |
| 1984 | 2,001.0 |
| 1988 | 1,740.0 |
| 1989 | 1,750.0 |
| 1991 | 2,050.0 |

Sources: Calculated from *Statistical Yearbook of Jamaica*, 1981, 1983, 1990, 1991; *Economic and Social Survey*, 1983, 1991.

population, which occurred at the beginning of the new decade. That population increase, especially in the younger age cohorts, did serve to lessen the statistical impact of crime in the society, even though raw or aggregate numbers of serious crime had either actually increased or remained relatively constant. Toward the end of the 1980s, and on into the 1990s, the crime rate moved upward as the population base either stabilized or dipped slightly (because of, say, outmigration) and as the aggregate number of crimes also increased (*see* table 2).

A cursory examination of the most recent (i.e., 1992) figures shows a countrywide persistence in high levels of violent crime. Six-hundred and twenty-nine murders were recorded for 1992, compared with 561 in 1991, according to Deputy Commissioner's report cited in *The Sunday Gleaner* of January 3, 1993.[19] All of the violent street crimes (assault, rape, and robbery), however, showed a 7 percent decrease in 1992, going down by 537 to 7,221 over the 7,758 reported in 1991. Two-hundred and sixty, or 42 percent, of the 629 murders recorded in 1992 were classified as "domestic." Of the others, 150, or 24 percent, were associated with robberies, break-ins, and rapes. Reprisal or revenge was the motive in 92, or 15 percent, of all the known homicides; and killings relating to mob violence, drugs, politics, and gang feuds accounted for 120, or 19 percent. In addition to the 629 street and domestic murders, 135 people were killed by the security forces in 1992; and twenty-one more were shot by private security guards.

The number of rape cases for 1992 was 596, a decline of 45 percent over 1991's total of 1,091. In 69 percent of all reported rape cases for 1992, the victims—who were in all instances female—knew their male attacker.

A total of 3,741, or 52 percent, of the street crimes reported to the police in 1992 involved the use of guns. Use of high-powered weapons (mostly semiautomatics) to commit robberies increased by some 12 percent over the previous year.

During 1992, continues the *Gleaner*'s summary of the Police Commissioner's report, the security forces destroyed 1,720 acres of *ganja* (or marijuana) plants, 270,345 *ganja* seedlings, and fourteen *ganja* nurseries; confiscated 69,376 pounds of cured *ganja*, 4,290 *ganja* balls, and fifty pounds of *ganja* seeds; and seized 1,445 pounds of cocaine, 691 pieces of crack cocaine, three one-quarter pounds of heroin, and 365 pounds of hash oil, a derivative of *ganja*.

Six-thousand two-hundred and ninety-eight persons were arrested in 1992 for possession of, dealing in, and exporting illegal drugs and other controlled substances. Of those arrested, 1,840 were foreigners, most of them apprehended at the island's two international airports.

A significant factor responsible for the persistence of high levels of violent crime in the first three years of the 1990 decade was the return of a number of the island's "exported" criminals who had left the country in the previous decade. A more thorough discussion of these "re-exportees" follows in chapter two. Eight-hundred and fifty-four Jamaicans living abroad with known international crime connections were deported back to Jamaica in 1992. They were sent mostly from Canada, Great Britain, and, more often than not, from the United States. This brought the total number of Jamaicans who were forcibly returned home from the metropolitan North between 1987 and 1992 because of their known or alleged criminal activities to 3,524. Mostly, according to the Jamaican authorities, these deportees were sent home because of weapons charges or because they had been involved in the sale and distribution of narcotics.

One set of these returning felons would be more criminally well-connected than when they had first left the island. Characteristic of their return-to-Jamaica lifestyle would be overt displays of "donmanship" and flaunting of ill-gotten items of conspicuous consumption—flashy automobiles and flamboyant styles of dress, for instance. They would become menacing, haunting bearers of a furtive "morality" that emphasized quick and easy routes for attaining material success symbols. Another set of returning offenders would come back finding themselves more destitute and more alienated from the society. They would be added to the ranks of an already massive urban lumpen proletariat or underclass. The two sets of returnees would, however, share an outcast fate. And the island's security forces would attribute a "new wave" of crime, violence, and terror (most of it tied to the international narcotics trade) to these unwanted youngsters, those whom many had thought the society had somehow ridded itself.

The bottom line is this: although actual crime figures may suffer from endemic reporting/recording irregularities, crime, particularly violent crime, is an insistent feature of the Jamaican society. Analysis of its root causes requires clear-headed thinking, if not always dispassionate "objectivity." This leads to a discussion of the overall theoretical and ideological lens through which I view Jamaica's crime problem.

## Theoretical Starting Point

Basically, I am viewing crime and violence in the Jamaican society, and among overseas Jamaicans, as societal phenomena: that is, as a type of activity whose manifestation pertains to certain objective features—social, political, economic, and to some extent cultural—in the ordering of the Jamaican society.

These features, by their very nature, do not, obviously, reside solely within the individual or in one's face-to-face or primary interactions. Consequently, the violence between, say, husband and wife, sweetheart and lover, or between friends, or over a card or domino game, however extreme the outcome, must be viewed as an entirely different phenomenon from the violence of a robbery, the wholesale killing of political opponents, or the gunning down of drug-trade rivals. The difference lies not just in number of people killed or degree of force used, but in source and aetiology. Some violent acts may result from "weird" individual pathology, whereas others are more clearly related to prevailing social-structural imperatives. Let me elaborate.

Violence pertaining to individual pathologies tends to fall loosely into two distinct types. One is a sort of primeval violence in which the perpetrators derive some warped satisfaction from the act of violence, in and of itself. Or they may find joyous release through the sheer act of beating up or torturing someone. People who beat up or kill prostitutes, children, and other victims who pose no conceivable threat to them are examples of this extreme type of *individualized*—yet purely impersonal—violent tendency. Known criminal cases in which the accused was said to have shown this type of violence would include serial killers, such as Great Britain's "Jack the Ripper" and Boston's Albert DeSalvo, the "Boston Strangler."

Also included in this "family" of habitual or repeat killers would be cases of *mass* slayings[20]—for example, Los Angeles' Charles Manson, whose cultlike followers went on a killing spree of Hollywood celebrities in 1969; Chicago's Richard Speck, who in a single episode in the summer of 1966 strangled and stabbed eight student nurses; and Jamaica's own Thaddeus Hyatt, who in the early 1960s went on a murderous rampage, chopping up an entire family, including young babies. Behaviourists (typically psychologists and psychoanalysts) refer to both sets of killers as individuals with a deranged psychopathic streak, or as psychopaths.[21] Blood, mayhem, sexual torture, and slow death give them strange, incomprehensible pleasure. They are, therefore, likely to attack or kill any vulnerable person.

The other type of *individualized* violence is directly personal and intimate. Satisfaction comes from meting out aggression (or vengeance) toward a specific or named person. Included here would be cases of domestic violence, in which fulfillment comes from the physical intimidation, or even annihilation, of a *known* antagonist—from, say, the mauling of a spouse, lover, or friend. Violence of this sort is used, some would say, to validate one's personal power over his/her victim.[22] The aggressor seeks nothing more than the victim's "respect" or "recognition," even if that recognition comes, finally, from standing over the victim's lifeless body. Individuals who derive their satisfactions in such an unusual manner suffer from all types of behavioural disorders, say the psychologists.

Indeed all modern—and postmodern—societies must inevitably contend with varying levels of both impersonal and personal types of individualized violence. Some societies have gone so far as to implement ritualized provisions for the "acting out" of these typically male-oriented violent symptoms. The Swiss and the Japanese, for example, have sanctioned an assortment of primal-scream outlets for displacement of violent fits and power wishes.

The one essential characteristic of all acts of individualized violence is that they are, for the most part, private and individually centered (i.e., psychological). Their occurrence, however frequent, upsetting, and distasteful, signals no real danger or coming apart at the seams in the social contract. Among other things, they do not have an impact on the lives of millions of people; neither do they reveal some essential truth about society.

Not so with street or conventional crimes, which do inhere more serious consequences for long-term structural harm. Most street crimes, such as robbery, are not really motivated by any complicated psychological abstraction. Instead, they become a tool in the service of achieving some "higher" objective. That objective can be to (1) obtain money, food, or other usable items; (2) control political or drug turf; or (3) physically control and/or dominate an entire class of actors, as in the crime of rape, about which I should say more.

The once widely held view that rape is a crime of male passion and, hence, a symptom of some psychological disorder is now largely discredited. A more enlightened view has emerged in recent years; it is the view that rape is a consequence of the unequal relationship of power between the sexes. Thus, the sole intent of the rapist, who typically is male, is to subdue. Rape is thus a way of validating male sexual *and* social power over women. Deviant sexual gratification plays a minimal motivational role, if any, in male rape crimes, argue feminist authors such as Susan Brownmiller. She posits, instead, that rape is a crime of violence and power over women. Throughout history, Brownmiller writes, rape has played a critical function in male domination. "It is nothing more or less than a conscious process of intimidation, by which all men keep all women in a state of fear."[23] Writer Marcia Ann Gillespie makes a similar point. "Too many people still confuse the rape of an adult woman with sex," she writes. "They don't see it for what it really is—a crime of dominance and degradation."[24]

Street killings, rape, robbery, and other forms of objectified or *structural* violence do, indeed, restrict the possibilities for cooperative social relations. It is this class of criminal acts that is the bane of modern Jamaica—and of America's inner cities. I shall henceforth refer to them as violent street-level crimes.

## Street Crimes' Distinctive Feature

In trying to explain the aetiology, or cause, of *all* street-level crimes in Jamaica, we should first try to place them within some sort of social-structural dynamic.

Most street crimes in Jamaica are generally of a depersonalized nature, since, usually, the assailant consciously suspends whatever personal or firsthand knowledge, if any, he may have of his victim. Actual names and faces of victims are, thus, objectively less important than the social or material gains (expected and actual) derived from the use of violence. Taking another look at the preliminary figures for 1992, we see, for instance, that more than half of all the island's murders (i.e., outside of the 42 percent domestic homicides) suggest situations in which issues other than purely interpersonal disputes dominated. In other words, well over 50 percent of all murders were associated with robberies, burglaries (or break-ins), gang violence, drugs, or political warfare. The majority of the island's killings, the figures show, *do not* involve situations which prior firsthand or intimate knowledge between victim and offender played a major role.

One additional examination of these figures, particularly as they relate to robbery, helps make my larger theoretical point about the depersonalized/property implications of most street crimes in Jamaica. The primary intent of a robbery is, of course, to separate the victim from his/her property; the accompanying violence is generally secondary. Robbery is, therefore, primarily a property crime. When we examine the figures for 1991 (the last year for which we have firm numbers), we find that of the eight specifically named violent street crimes, robbery accounted for a huge 60 percent of all such crimes. (Homicide, or murder, accounted for a much smaller, though by no means negligible, 6 percent.) Moreover, when the numbers for all reported street crimes—violent and property—for that year are combined, robbery leads the pack, accounting for a significant 25 percent of *all* listed (sixteen in all) non–"white-collar" crimes.

The upshot is this: the gunman who robs, and perhaps in the process kills, the downtown shopkeeper or white North American tourist typically holds no particular personal grudge against either victim. In carrying out his crime, the robber/gunman sees the victim as a removable, depersonalized obstruction who stands between him and some larger prize.

The same basic rationale holds true for drug wars. Competitors are eliminated, "dropped," "smoked," or "iced" not because of personality differences or failure to communicate, as say in a marriage, but because they represent threats, real or imagined, to another's maximum control over the sale and marketing of a lucrative commodity. So, also, are instances of political "tribal" warfare among Jamaica's rival political gangs (discussed in the following chapter), where the faceless, unnamed poor and dispossessed become "cannon fodder"—to use Professor Nettleford's apt terminology—in the dogfight for partisan political supremacy.

Victims, whether they are tourists, shopkeepers, innocent householders, drug-trade competitors, political foes, or vulnerable women, all become expendable targets in a larger, fiercer "struggle" for goods, status, money, and power. A preponderance in cases of street-level criminal violence usually indicates some deep-rooted pathology *within the social system.*[25] Violence of the strictly street variety cannot be eradicated by applying essentially individualized corrective measures, such as simply locking up offenders, as necessary as that is most times, or by making episodic police sweeps and raids on *ganja* dealers, however good it might make government feel.

All street-level crime and the criminals' tendency toward violence are problems which, if their root causes are left structurally unattended to, will reproduce themselves. Their underlying source is arithmetic growth in the size of an at-risk population that is faced with precious few alternatives to crime. Thus, for every "Johnny-Too-Bad" the Jamaican state imprisons—something it has been doing quite well over the years, to the point that the prisons are now overcrowded—probably ten new alienated little "Johnny-Too-Bads" are being reproduced everyday to take his place.

The cause of all street-level crime and violence, then, must be found in the nature of the society itself, not in the mental or emotional states of its citizens. Neither can the crimes be simple-mindedly dismissed as purely acts of greed and envy coming from "wicked" and "bad mind" people. If the explanation for crime in Jamaica is "born wickedness," then the Jamaican people might do well to ask, "Why is it that the country has had successive generations of *so many* 'wicked' people?" A couple of "freaks" here and there might seem reasonable, but going back to the 1940s and the days of the legendary Rhygin,[26] the society has been throwing up, fairly steadily, waves of rogues, desperados, and badmen over the course of the most recent years; however, the activities of these rogues and badman have become more brutal and more depersonalized.

Official explanations of high levels of Jamaican crime being the doings of a certain class of inherently "evil" people must be taken for what they are: backward and reactionary. Babies do not come into the world brandishing an Uzi, a MAC-10, a Tek9, an Ingram, or a Cobray M-11/9 (all powerful assault artillery in the drug underworld) in one hand and a lighted "spliff" in the other. Widespread acceptance of the notion of "born criminals," and of the "animalness" of some Jamaicans, has served over the years to justify and encourage the actual physical elimination, by the island's public and private security forces among others, of an entire segment of the society's population.

But what exactly is it in the Jamaican society—in its history, culture, politics, and development—that produces and reproduces the motivated offender, the people who disregard the laws of society, in fact feel no part of society, and so go out and commit unspeakable atrocities on others? That question we shall grapple with next.

# 2
# From Whence Did "We" Get Such People?

*We make life really terrible for some people*
*and then blame them when they become dangerous.*
—Norval Morris

In the preceding chapter, I tried to set forth a typology of crime and violence in the Jamaican society. I suggested that, by and large, violent street crime in Jamaica is essentially depersonalized. That is, in the commission of a violent criminal act, assailants are not usually motivated or driven by some weird, primeval instinct. I argued, instead, that much of Jamaica's street-level violence has social-structural implications in that it is mostly directed toward obtaining socially approved objects such as money, goods, status, or power. Most crimes are committed because they procure "certain advantages," writes the French philosopher Michel Foucault.[1] The unfortunate person who stands between the gunman and his objective becomes, to put it crudely, expendable.

The root causes, then, for the alarmingly high levels of Jamaican street crime are in the nature of a society that either withholds or denies possession of prized objects from a significant number of its citizens, not in the mental states of the thousands of "Johnny-Too-Bads" the nation regularly imprisons, ships abroad, sends to the Spanish Town gallows, or otherwise executes through various extra-legal means.

So the underlying question I will address here is this: whence did "we" get all these bad people? These people who roam the streets night and day, "scaring the nation with their guns and ammunition"; people who break into other people's homes and cars and take their possessions; people who cold-bloodedly murder loved ones; who seem literally to thrive on rivalry and gangsterism; who do nothing but wreak havoc and mayhem on an otherwise blessed country; people who, finally, take their misdeeds abroad and there wreak more havoc and mayhem, only to be re-exported back home to continue (or start all over again) a life of waste, death, and destruction. From whence do these people come?

The answer, to quote the Belgian criminologist Adolphe Quetelet, is that society carries within itself, in some sense, the seeds of all crimes which are going to be committed, together with the facilities for their development."[2] Put less cumbersomely, society gets the criminals it produces—and perhaps deserves.

Having said this, let me hasten to add that, unlike some of my more "radical" colleagues,[3] I share no romantic notion of the hoodlum in Jamaica. I do not see him (and it's usually a *him*) as some sort of revolutionary "don." The tendency in some Leftist circles to glorify crime as "primitive rebellion" and to interpret it as a form of spontaneous, anti-capitalist revolt is, I believe, misguided. Although we can find some support for the idea of crime as revolt in earlier historical epoches, both in Jamaica and in the "developed" West, that is generally not the case today. Social banditry was then a form of class struggle and often a precursor or accompaniment to peasant uprisings.[4]

But the street-level crimes carried out by Jamaican posses and assorted thugs bear no resemblance, none whatsoever, to the social banditry of the Sicilian peasants, to the uprisings of the dislocated farmers of Central Asia, to the rebellion of the rural poor in mercantilist England, or to the killings of British slave hunters by Jamaican Maroons. "Bandits" and "badmen" in the contemporary Jamaican setting are more likely to rip off and kill fellow *sufferahs* and hold up the struggling businessman than they are to attack the citadels of genuinely exploitative capital. Violent crimes in Jamaica must, therefore, be seen for what they essentially are: the parasitical, reactionary activity of generations of the society's urban disaffected.

Such a reading, however, begs the central question: how did Jamaica get its disaffected, its urban lumpen proletariat? And is their generational persistence in the social order completely unexpected, a surprise? Or is it a logical outgrowth of the country's sociohistorical and socio-economic processes?

In what follows I shall try to explain, first, the rise and perpetuation of a disaffected, wageless, nonworking class within the Jamaican society, the class whose members account for the vast majority of all reported street crime. Next I shall explore the relationship between street crime, drug trafficking, guns, and politics among the country's poor and non-working class. Finally, I will attempt a tentative explanation system for the exportation to the United States, and re-exportation back to Jamaica, of known Jamaican criminal elements.

The explanation system I shall propose can be summarized in terms of the following six propositions.

- Over the course of the last thirty or so years (from about the mid-1960s to the present), the coalescing of various contradictory forces in the Jamaican society has resulted in the formation of a distinct urban lumpen proletariat of youthful males for whom street crime and involvement in a subterranean, illegal drug economy have become normal, functional enterprises.

- Growth in the 1970s and 1980s of an international narcotics market, coupled with waves of political unrest in the Caribbean, coincided with an even greater increase in the size of Jamaica's urban wageless class. Several within this class would find ready, lucrative "employment" in, among other illegal activities, the illegal drug trade emanating from places such as Miami and New York, in gun dealing and in "ordinary" street crime.
- Integration of Jamaican "elements" into the international narcotics trade was facilitated by high international demand (mainly in the United States) for Jamaica's own "high grade" cannabis (known locally as *ganja*); whereas integration into international gun running and political thuggery were facilitated by a process of mutual exploitation between local politicians and some of the island's leading thugs.
- As Jamaica's conventional criminal elements grew, they increasingly became more unmanageable. Significant numbers of them would leak through the local immigration and criminal justice cracks and eventually obtain travel documents to the metropolitan countries.
- It is the exportation (or outmigration) of significant numbers of the country's criminal elements that accounts, in part, for the posse phenomenon; the other part lies in the facts of dispossession of first-generation Jamaicans (the "Jamericans") *in* the United States.
- In the years to follow, notably in the late 1980s through early 1990s, many within the class of outmigrating offenders would be forcibly returned to Jamaica, after being either suspected or convicted of crimes in the United States. Restart of their criminal careers in Jamaica would constitute a new dimension to the island's crime problem.

I shall return to these propositions in a moment, but first let's look briefly at the people behind prison bars in Jamaica. Such an examination can give us a clue as to the common circumstances that conceivably "drive" some people in the society into crime. (Incidentally, such an examination can also give insights into the workings of the Jamaican justice system—for example, which types of offences and offenders the authorities are most likely to punish.)

## The People Behind Jamaica's Prison Bars

Some years ago I was able to talk with and interview a fairly representative sample of Jamaica's incarcerated.

Of the 3,000 or so people in the nation's maximum security prisons back in the mid-1980s, all were virtually penniless, except, that is, for a few drug-dealing "Mr. Bigs." Most owned no real assets. Before being imprisoned, they had little access, if any, to the basic necessities of life—things such as a regular meal and a sure place to sleep. They had no real work-related skills. In fact, two-thirds of them were basically illiterate. More than 80 percent of them had never held a steady job at the time of either their arrest or rearrest, half of them never having so much as experienced a single day of honest work in their entire adult lifetimes. Entire prison populations were basically young; 70 percent of all first-time offenders in one prison were between the ages of eighteen and twenty-nine. Ninety percent and more of all those incarcerated were males, 99.9 percent of whom were Afro-Jamaicans. Not so surprising is the latter, one might say, in a society of 2.4 million where more than 85 percent of the population are the direct "unmixed" descendants of African slaves. When seen, however, against the background that the country also has within its midst noticeable numbers of "other" racial or racially mixed groupings (some 15 percent), that 99.9 percent Afro-Jamaicans in prison seems rather unfavourably skewed.[5]

Before their entanglement with the law, most inmates in the older age groups (i.e., over thirty years old) had never participated in any meaningful way in the nation's political process, except for maybe voting in a general election or two, or at some time or another being party to armed partisan conflict. Equally disturbing was that more than 60 percent of all inmates I talked with had at least one prior conviction, even if they had not all been incarcerated or actually served time before.

Finally, Jamaica's imprisoned came disproportionately from the most disadvantaged or slum areas of the island's urban centres, more than half of them coming from within, or just outside, the greater Kingston area. Rarely did the most violent repeat offenders come (at least not directly) from the rural, close-knit, traditional settings of "the country." Most repeat offenders, in other words, came primarily from the nation's "concrete jungles" and its "Back O'Walls."

What do these facts mean? They mean that the people who end up in the society's penal institutions are a compressed, homogenized lot. They all look alike. They further tell us that the people whom the Jamaican state spends large sums of money annually to *lock up* represent a significant portion of the people who are *locked out* of the society[6]—namely the black youthful males whom the nation's political, economic, and educational systems have consistently failed. The people who actually end up behind Jamaican prison bars are from among Barbadian writer George Lamming's people "from below." They are people for whom, borrowing from a quotation of the philosopher Arthur Schopenhauer, frequently cited by Martin Luther King, Jr., in his speeches, "life is an endless pain with a painful end." They are people who have lost hope and have nothing to look forward to. They represent, in novelist Upton Sinclair's evocative description of life for turn-of-the-twentieth-century East European

Chicago immigrants, "the drainage of the great festering ulcer of society; hideous to look upon, sickening to talk to. All life had turned to rottenness and stench in them—love a beastliness, joy a snare, and God an imprecation."[7] For the contemporary imprisoned in Jamaica, the nation's flag, its pretensions to greatness, charm and beauty, its national anthem and claims of solidarity with international liberation struggles are all like "tinkling cymbals" (in the words of the Apostle Paul) and "full of sound and fury, signifying nothing" (to quote Shakespeare's Macbeth).

Among those for whom life on the outside was a continuous tangle with the police, I found cynicism and distrust of the nation's civic and political leaders, of its intelligentsia and economic elites. The imprisoned—who undoubtedly at some point *did* break some law and perhaps *did* violate someone—were folks, I found, on the "outside" of society who ask in the simmering spirit of the African-American patriot, Frederick Douglas, *What does "your" independence mean to us, except for a never-ending stream of silly festival songs and beauty contests?*

As one angry "Johnny-Too-Bad" pressed me, from behind the uncertain safety afforded by the prison bars that separated us, "Wha more dem can do me? So mi commit murder and dem 'ang mi? But, *rass*! out deh [on the streets], mi 'ready dead." He was, of course, referring not just to the possibility of death at the hands of fellow outcasts—or of the security forces, an equally likely possibility—but to the daily reality of his own existential and material death. His lament was not an expression of greed, envy, or wickedness. Rather, it was born of hopelessness, despair, and a sense of powerlessness in the capacity to shape positively the course of *his* biography. That kind of despair renders many Jamaican youngsters vulnerable to "employment" in the narcotics trade, turns them into street hoodlums, or makes them fair game for predatory politicians. The lure of dubious status positions either within the drug underworld or on the darker side of Jamaican politics (or both) can be a mighty tempting thing to otherwise unfulfilled, desperate lives.

## Structural Reasons for Jamaica's "Crime-Disposed" or "At Risk" Population

The rise of a disaffected lumpen proletariat (those who make up what middle-class Jamaicans like to call the "hooligan element") is neither mysterious nor unexpected. Some years ago I argued that to understand the root causes of crime in Jamaica, we must first understand how certain structural, historical forces in the society have shaped the formation of a peculiarly "at risk" segment of the population, for whom involvement in crime becomes a normal and indeed functional activity.[8] In fact, for many within the Jamaican "underclass" (to invoke a discredited term), crime is an enterprise. Most times it is the only *available* enterprise.

The creation of an urban nonworking or wageless class, I shall argue, is a logical outgrowth of Jamaica's socioeconomic and historical processes. Three major interrelated forces are responsible for the growth of the country's "at-risk" or "crime-disposed" population:

- the decline of agricultural production, which led to, among other things, massive internal and (later) external migration;
- evolution of a disarticulated modern economy; and
- steady, continuous increases in the rate of growth in the youthful age cohorts without sufficient base for their productive absorption into the economy.

Until the early 1830s, the Jamaican economy was dominated by the sugar plantation. After the Emancipation Proclamation of August 1, 1834, which formally freed the slaves in the British colonial West Indies, the Jamaican plantation system declined as a source of primary accumulation. Further eroding the Jamaican planter class's once virtual monopoly on the world sugar market were competition from new plantations of European sugar beet, establishment of the continental system, and the ending of tariff and subsequent promotion of freer trade.

After emancipation, the planters tried every possible scheme to keep the ex-slaves tied to the plantations. In reality, the slaves were not actually freed in 1834; instead, they became "apprentices" obliged to perform forty-and-a-half hours of unpaid labour each week. The freed slaves were outraged by this hypocrisy and rioted violently, bringing to an end, in 1838, this exploitative apprenticeship system. Everywhere throughout the colonial Caribbean, freed slaves looked for ways to leave the hated plantations and become economically independent. But it was in Jamaica (and also Guyana), where land was relatively abundant, that the fullest development of a free black peasant society flourished. Under pressure from the planters, the British government would sell land only in large tracts so as to keep the ex-slaves from buying. But the freed slaves circumvented this restriction by pooling their savings and buying land jointly, either forming cooperatives or parcelling out individual plots to families. Missionary societies also purchased land for the ex-slaves. By 1865, two-thirds of Jamaica's freed slaves had basically left the sugar plantations and were living in free villages, many of them situated on precarious hillsides.

No real integrated system of agricultural production emerged to replace sugar as the primary employer. Subsistence and peasant farming served to supplement irregular incomes earned from the remaining plantations. In 1850, the percentage of the labour force engaged in this dual agricultural activity was 71 percent; in 1880 it fell to 67 percent, and it was still over half in 1930. But in the relatively short span of thirteen years between 1930 and 1943, the percentage of people in all forms of agricultural production fell to under 44 percent. In 1990 that figure was less than 30 percent.

As people moved out of agriculture, they were supposed to move, following economist Arthur Lewis's model, into the newer areas of Jamaica's modern economy. The modern Jamaican economy emerged in the 1950s, with the growth of foreign investment in bauxite and alumina production,[9] manufacturing, and tourism. It was in these new economic sectors that people were supposed to find employment. But one of the crucial relationships in the country's economic history has always been the size and demographic character of people in the labour force in relation to the available jobs in the modern economic sector. Ever since the 1950s, a disparity has existed between the consequences of the annual rate of natural increase of the population (between 2 and 3 percent) and the capacity of the economic structure to absorb those no longer able to find work in agriculture—in other words, the classic development problem of too many people chasing too few jobs. Jamaica's population grew steadily between 1940 and 1980—from just under 1 million in 1940 to 2.4 million at the end of 1990. In each of the years between 1940 and the mid-1980s, the country threw up into the labour pool considerably more people than the economy was able to provide jobs for. Naturally, the majority of these new job seekers were in the crucial eighteen- to twenty-five-year-old age group. On average, for each of the years between 1980 and 1989, some 40,000 youngsters graduated from the nation's post-elementary schools. Another 8,000 or so young adults came out of the teacher colleges; the College of Arts, Science, and Technology (CAST); West Indies College; the Mona campus of the University of the West Indies (UWI); and from commercial/technical schools. The numbers could hardly have been considered overwhelming or "explosive" relative to population size, since throughout the 1980s the overall size of the population in the sixteen- to twenty-four-year-old age group stood at around 450,000.[10] The 40,000 or so who in each of those years were fortunate enough to have acquired some limited skill or education beyond elementary school still had precious few occupational or career places to go within the nation's economy.

From the end of the 1960s through the end of the 1980s, the local economy was able to absorb no more than one-fifth of *all* new job seekers, schooled and unschooled, per year. The economy's manufacturing, public service, bauxite, and tourist sectors had simply not generated enough new jobs. Thus consistently left behind, year after year, was a massive pool of "surplus" or unemployed youths who had to find alternate ways to fend for themselves.[11] Worse, even after completing some form of schooling, a significant number of job seekers had not really acquired essential job-related skills, notwithstanding significant improvements in the country's overall educational system in the years leading up to and immediately following the granting of political independence, in 1962.[12] So even if there had been enough jobs to go around, many of the island's youngsters would not have been qualified to fill them.

## The Migration Option

One traditional way for dealing with the country's surplus-labour problem has always been outmigration, that is, government unofficially (and sometimes officially) encouraging the country's excess people to leave the land of their birth, to go "a foreign."

Jamaicans have been leaving home for a long time—for so long, in fact, and in such vast numbers, that today more than half of the world's estimated five million Jamaicans live outside their native land.[13] A passing look at the number of Jamaicans in the United States, alone, is instructive.

According to U.S. census data, from 1961 through 1970, 71,000 Jamaicans obtained permanent U.S. resident status. From 1971 through 1980, 142,000 did the same; so did another 213,000 between 1981 and 1990.[14] (These numbers, of course, do not reflect the thousands more who entered the American mainland on temporary visas then overstayed or the unknown numbers of "undocumenteds.") In 1980, 197,000 U.S. census respondents indicated Jamaica as their place of birth; in 1990, 343,000 made that claim, for an increase of 74 percent. Jamaicans constituted, in 1990, almost 2 percent of the U.S. foreign-born population. In 1980, 253,000 native-born Americans claimed immediate Jamaican ancestry; 435,000 (an increase of 72 percent) did so in 1990.[15]

Massive outmigration is part of a continuing historical trend for Jamaicans. The movement of Jamaicans away from home began almost as soon as slavery ended, when a relatively small number of Jamaicans, numbering in the hundreds, set sail for nearby ports in and around the Caribbean. Starting in the 1880s, thousands crossed the Caribbean Sea to Central America, where they cultivated bananas for United Fruit Company's plantations, built Costa Rica's railways, and dug the Panama Canal. When canal construction ended in 1914 and crop disease forced production cutbacks on the plantations, Jamaicans streamed into Cuba's sugar-cane fields and to northern industrial centers in the United States. In the forty years between 1881 and 1921 emigration carried off 156,000 Jamaicans, 35 percent of the period's total population increase.[16] Yet even the largest of these early migrations pale in comparison to the massive movement abroad at the end of the second World War, when twice as many Jamaicans abandoned their "Island in the Sun." Between 1948 and 1968, some 300,000 Jamaicans emigrated legally to Great Britain, Canada, and the United States; tens of thousands more, denied legal entry, chose undocumented existence in the slums of Brooklyn and Brixton over life in Jamaica.

Why, historically, have so many Jamaicans left, and continue to leave, home? The underlying answer gets back, inevitably, to Jamaica's longstanding, umbilical relationship to the sugar industry. I briefly explore this relationship below.[17] Eventually, I will tie this all together to show the historical role played by the plantation in effecting increases in levels of crime.

Following the emancipation of the slaves, the sugar industry underwent three profound changes, each of which had direct implications for the movement and subsequent outmigration of the Jamaican people.

### *Former Slaves Chose Subsistence Farming Over Cane Production*

The first change, as I already mentioned, was that the former slaves, who were now "free" to earn subsistence wages, used the proceeds of their meagre earnings to buy land on the country's hilly interior. Soon several of them were able to move away from the plantations altogether and become independent producers of small-scale foodstuffs—cassava, yams, sweet potato, and so forth. These were all foods for immediate, local consumption, as opposed to the export-oriented, single-crop production of sugar cane. In effect, several former slaves had thus committed the first act of mass exit: they left the confines of the estate to become peasant farmers. But peasant farming, although good for the self-esteem and sense of relative independence it provided the small farmer, created a problem for the plantation owner. It denied him one of the indispensables of capital: a controllable, "disciplined," economically dependent labouring class. For a time, plantation owners were successful in imposing a system of land tenancy. The drawback of this system was, however, that the plantation owners had to accept irregular, grab-bag–type wage work from a transient work force. Workers would simply pop in and out of sugar production as they damned well pleased. Needless to say, these and other arrangements could not sustain sugar at its once commanding slavery-days heights. In fact, the new set of circumstances were downright disastrous for the plantation owners.

Between 1848 and 1881 the number of estates operating in Jamaica plummeted—from 513 to 211—as owners sold out, packed up, and returned for good to Britain. This had a disastrous impact on the thousands of freed slaves who had not been able to purchase land and, consequently, depended on wage labour on the estates for a livelihood. They were now left without any real means to support themselves. One result of this process was that land capture escalated (the modern "Rasta" was, therefore, not the first at the practice). The more significant development, however, was that these early dislocated Jamaicans would start the move into the island's urban areas in search of new forms of wage labour. Eventually, as internal rural-urban migration proved unproductive, many of these new urban dwellers would be among the first to start the trek to distant ports around the Caribbean—north to Guantanamo and Havana, Cuba; and south to Colon, Panama; Limon, Costa Rica; Caracas, Venezuela; Bluefields, Nicaragua; and all along the British Honduran coast.

But also responsible for the massive movement in and eventually out of the island was monopoly capitalization of the sugar industry in the early years of the twentieth century.

*When the British Landowners Left, Large Corporations Moved In*

The second change came with the departure of several of the independent landowning class to Great Britain, thus clearing the way for the entrance of giant American and British corporations into the Jamaican sugar and other large-scale agricultural industries, such as banana and coffee. Enter companies such as the United Fruit Company of the United States and Great Britain's Tate & Lyle.

To maximize profits, these conglomerates also desired a pliant, "reliable" labour force. To get the type of work force they wanted, the companies quickly foreclosed on loans made to peasant and hillside farmers after hurricanes had destroyed their crops. The farmers, now forced off their land, had little choice but to come down from the hills and work for cheap wages in sugar production. In the meantime, the island's population was rapidly increasing and soil erosion was taking place on the hillsides where the remaining peasant farmers were trying to eke out a livelihood.

The situation was ripe for strife and mass disorder. It came in 1938, when the island was convulsed by a labour rebellion so profound that it forced the start of the process of decolonization. At the heart of the rebellion was a demand for increased wages and land reform. The Crown's response was a piecemeal land-settlement programme that did nothing to alleviate the country's land hunger. Britain's King George VI (Queen Elizabeth II's father) soon found out that he could suppress cries for economic justice by engaging the island's two most prominent nationalist leaders, Alexander Bustamante and Norman Washington Manley, in discussions over alternate forms of a revised system of colonial domination. Eventual political independence was, however, the goal of both leaders, whom a grateful nation would later honour as national heroes. But while the nationalist bourgeoisie clamoured for independence, the people who had started the rebellion still remained landless and hungry. To improve their circumstances, they would have to pull up what little stakes they had and move. Some, following their freed-slave forebearers, would make their move into the country's urban areas, where they would further swell the ranks of unemployed city dwellers. Others would leave the island, lock, stock and saltfish barrel.

*The Sugar Cane Industry Underwent Modernization*

Finally, in their continued drive to increase profits, major sugar companies, such as the West Indies Sugar Company (WISCO), embarked, in the 1950s, on a major programme of modernizing the industry and finding new ways to increase productivity. First, they created a registered work force, ending once and for all the troublesome system of workers popping in and out of the labour pool. If a worker was not on the registry, he or she could not work. Then they brought in mechanical loaders (nicknamed "the grab"), which in effect made thousands of cane hands redundant. Finally, they introduced the practice of crop-burning: that is, forty-eight hours before the cane is due for harvesting, the entire canepiece would be set on fire. The stated purpose of crop-burning was to reduce the water content of the cane, leaving a richer sucrose content, but its *real* purpose was to make the cane easier for cutting, thus reducing, by more than half, the number of hands needed.

The net results of these combined processes made sugar once again King—at least for the transnational corporations and local capitalist concerns such as J. Wray & Nephew. Sparked even further by new market guarantees and a surge in world market prices, between 1943 and 1953, the price of sugar jumped 170 percent. Profitability in the industry continued its upward spiral into 1965, when the world price of sugar took a nose-dive from which it never recovered.

But even in its heyday, workers had never really benefited from sugar, notwithstanding incremental wage increases due to strong union demands. In fact, the more rationalized and capital-intensive the industry became, the more people it displaced. Where would these displaced persons go? And what would they do? They had no land to which they could return. Besides, many hillside landowners had sold their land to the newly arriving bauxite companies. In a "free" country, when all other avenues for survival are either closed, blocked, or nonexistent, people have the option to move, to pick up and start over again somewhere else. Many Jamaicans did just that. First, they moved to the cities of Kingston, Montego Bay, May Pen, Spanish Town. Here nascent manufacturing and tourism sectors were supposed to provide them with new types of work. But only for a scant few did the promise of nonagricultural wage employment actually materialize.

The disinherited who had moved into the urban areas could either stay there and swell the ranks of the *sufferahs*, or they could depart permanently—by any available means—for "foreign." And go "a foreign" Jamaicans did. We did so by the hundreds of thousands, mostly by exploiting regular channels, notably through the United States' and Canadian "guest worker" programmes, and by responding to Great Britain's invitation, in the 1950s, to come on over and help rebuild that country's ravaged postwar economy. (In 1962, Britain would abruptly slam the door shut to Jamaicans and other dark-skinned people from its erstwhile colonies.) Others would seek to escape hunger, deprivation, and limited opportunity after concocting the most elaborately conceived stories to tell "the man" at the U.S. and Canadian embassies.

So over the course of several generations, migration, first internal then external, evolved into the one real viable way out for Jamaicans trapped in rural poverty.

## Emergence of the "Scuffler" Class

Scarcity of regular jobs, or jobs at reasonable wages, condemned a substantial portion of the people who were unable to migrate to a life of low-income, own-account activity in street and market vending. They were left behind in the nation's burgeoning urban centres.[18] Several of these new urban dwellers were once engaged in handicrafts such as dress-making or skilled trades such as carpentry. Or they had been wage-earning (albeit sporadically) sugar-cane workers. They would all become displaced persons in the country's modern economy. The end result was a swelling of the ranks of what Ken Post calls the "scuffler" class,[19] which today (in 1993) crams the shantytowns of the Kingston–St. Andrew–Spanish Town area, where more than half the nation's 1990 population lives.

"Scuffling" is simply another way of referring to involvement in informal or secondary enterprises. The term has been associated with two ways of eking out an existence. First is the intermittent and marginal sale of labour power; second is finding supplements for maintaining one's self when regular work is either unavailable or inadequate. So occasional wage labour, grabbed when and where available, perhaps on the docks or at construction sites, frequently supplements income from "occupations" such as car-minding, casual messengering, "postering," postcard selling, sno-cone vending, finding parking spaces, opening doors, cleaning cars (or car windshields), shoe shining, and "hawking goods in infinitesimal quantities."[20]

Frequently, irregular income is also gained from illegalities such as petty larceny, housebreaking, stickups, prostitution, gun running, *ganja* trafficking, and becoming "top ranking" enforcers for corrupt politicians. These activities—along with the less-risky or honest ones, such as offers to wash cars—are all thrown into the mix of things one does to survive in an environment in which survival by other socially accepted means is not guaranteed.

Describing life among Kingston's disinherited in 1965, the Rev. W.A. Blake wrote the following:

> A great source of income was 'scuffling' and *ganja* was significant. Close the Coronation Market and Back O' Wall would be rapidly depopulated—the people there ate chiefly on Thursday, Friday and Saturday. . . . The effect on family would be illustrated by the case of a girl whose mother told her she could no longer feed her; the girl took to 'scuffling' for herself, and was often half-starved, became a prostitute, now at eighteen has a baby whose father is in prison.[21]

Blake's description of life among Kingston's dispossessed is even more true today, in 1993, than it was almost thirty years ago.

Communities in areas of, say, West Kingston have been, for the most part, deprived of the material-economic base whereby its members can reproduce and adequately maintain themselves. They are not only "truly disadvantaged"; they are truly powerless. In these environs people become "surplus" individuals and exist as a subproletariat who are "consigned" to a position of "wagelessness," to use Stuart Hall's apt phraseology.[22] Not having any hope of future employment, their life conditions have specific personal and social consequences, including a resort to crime. Criminologist Richard Quinney describes more fully below the dilemma of this urban subproletariat:

> Basic human needs are thwarted when the life-giving activity of work is lost or curtailed. . . . [Unemployment] means the loss of personal and family income. Choices, opportunities, and even life maintenance are jeopardized. For many people, the appropriate reaction consists not only of mental disturbance but also of outright acts of personal and social destruction. . . . Crimes of economic gain increase whenever the jobless seek ways to maintain themselves and their families. Crimes of violence rise when the problems of life are further exacerbated by the loss of life-supporting activity. Anger and frustration at a world that punishes rather than supports produce their own forms of destruction. Permanent unemployment—and the acceptance of that condition—can result in a form of life where criminality is an omnipresent response.[23]

Many crimes committed in Jamaica are responses to the material conditions inherent to economic dispossession, severe inequality, and general hopelessness. Disconnected youths who are powerless to change their bleak condition take advantage of the "opportunities" afforded by street crime. It is not ghetto or a violent subculture—or any other *internal* pathology—that impels them. Rather, it is the need to survive, to "exist in a society where survival is not assured by other, collective means," writes Quinney.[24] To sit around and dream and hope, as many do, only leads to further frustration. To just "hang out" on the corner and sulk, or run one's mouth, does in the long run prove unimaginative, not to mention unproductive. Neither one puts food in one's belly, pays the rent, buys baby food, or provides dancehall money. Neither will it outfit one in the preppy sports costumes, the fancy Reebok and Nike "kicks," so frequently seen in the stores and profiled on the affluent on the other side of town.

The uninitiated might chide: "Go find a job and you can have, and do, all of those things." But what job? Where are they? And with what credentials? For recognition, status, and hundreds of dollars a day, the more enterprising do find risky, short-lived employment in the criminal underground—as pushers, badmen, or political "dons." Denied all other options, including access to the lucrative narcotics trade and to political bosses, the youthful wretched of the land end up victimizing, by way of violent street crimes, their social-class opposites and, more often than not, those who like themselves are already socially victimized.

## Drugs, Guns, and Politics

The year 1960 saw 33,000 unemployed persons within Kingston's labour force, according to Terry Lacey.[25] He estimates that by 1971, "after further urbanization, severe restrictions on emigration and a rise in the general rate of unemployment to 25 percent," the number of unemployed persons in Kingston "would have had to be over 100,000." He continues:

> Given that the population of Kingston by 1970 was about 625,000 and that the non-working class had to 'support' a certain number of dependents. . ., it is reasonable to conclude that the lumpen proletariat comprised at least 150,000 persons, or approximately a quarter [the population] of Kingston.[26]

Hopeless poverty, frustration, and dispossession gave rise to militant Rastafarianism, black nationalism, and reggae music.[27] The lyrics of one early reggae song, by singer Bob Andy, illustrate the despair of youngsters coming to the city in search of work and finding none:

> This couldn't be my home
> It must be somewhere else
>
> Can't get no clothes to wear
> Can't get no food to eat
> Can't get a job to get bread . . .

But frustration also produced a type of misplaced, violent anger, its most frightening manifestations being glorification of a breed of ghetto young men hailed as "rude bways" and "Johnny-Too-Bads," and veneration of the well-connected gunman, the "top ranking." The lyrics of another late-1960s reggae song by singer Desmond Decker foretold of an oncoming, more fearsome *Zeitgeist*:

> Walkin' down the road with a pistol in yu waist
> Johnny, yu too bad
> Yu jus' shootin'
> An yu lootin'
> An yu stabbin'
> Bway, yu too bad.[28]

This anger and frustration in the late 1960s was ripe for opportunism and exploitation. Growth of an international illegal drug market provided the "opportunity," and local politicians did a lot of the exploiting.

Yvonne Satherswaite believes that the advent of an international trade in the Jamaican cannabis, *ganja*, developed as the result of two interrelated factors.[29] First, the joint efforts in the late 1960s and early 1970s of the Mexican–U.S. authorities to "clamp down" on the Mexican marijuana trade resulted in traders seeking out new supply sources. Second, the "unique quality" of Jamaican *ganja* allowed excellent blending with cannabis produced in other countries. So, as it turned out, Jamaica, with its relatively open borders and close proximity to the United States, also had, to boot, a product that was simply "out of this world." Added to all these "advantages," inside Jamaica was an army of angry, surplus youths who, having nothing to lose, would risk life and limb to move into the rich North American market not only Jamaican-grown *ganja* but cocaine coming from up from South America. Thus, began the integration of Jamaican elements into the illegal drug trade.

In the late 1970s, according to information looked at by anthropologist Faye Harrison, the illegal drug trade was "the only stable sector of [a] failing [local] economy."[30] Even former Prime Minister Edward Seaga, she writes, "admitted that when he entered office in 1980 marijuana production was 'the only healthy segment of the Jamaican economy.' The 1.1 billion dollar business [had] been the economic lifeline of Jamaica for years, especially after traditional segments of the economy failed."[31] The security forces could identify, in the early 1980s, some sixty to seventy illegal airstrips around the island. Light Cesna aircraft would land and, quick as a flash, motors still running, they would make their daily pickups and take off for the Florida coast. Patches of *ganja* were grown in urban gullies and on secluded uncultivated rural lands. By the middle of the decade Jamaica had earned the dubious reputation of being the second largest source for all marijuana entering the United States, second only to Columbia. In 1983, the island supplied 1,750 metric tons of *ganja* to the United States, according to the Jamaican government's own data.[32] The money made from all these transactions, including huge transshipments of cocaine, was indeed more than enough to have put a sizeable dent in the island's crushing debt and foreign-exchange burden.[33] Control of the local *ganja* "industry" rested with international cartels and local barons living in luxurious, splendid isolation along the island's fabulous north coast. But it was the trigger-happy "rude bways" of Kingston, working under the direction of the "top rankings," and the underpaid, easily bought police, who provided the muscle and saw to it that the merchandise was moved.

Gradually, drug peddling came to replace some street-crime activity—perhaps so because of street crimes' now relatively miniscule gains (after all, only *so much* could be stolen from fellow *sufferahs*) or because of their plain "oafishness," to borrow from Michael Thelwell.[34] Involvement in the drug trade not only offered lots of cash to youths who had never experienced a full day of legitimate work, but also it provided an opportunity to make connections with "big shot" people, including those who could spirit them abroad. But dealing in narcotics was dangerous business, a high-stakes gamble in which the life of every trader, particularly those dealing at the street level, was as expendable as that of the *maga dawg's*. Guns were needed for protection.

A curious concatenation of events brought the most sophisticated weaponry into the hands of the most insignificant underlings in the Jamaican underworld. Enter some of the island's leading politicians, who needed "safe seats," meaning, constituencies where voting results are always predictable—and in their favour. And the drug dealer needed guns. The guns would serve as tools of protection and intimidation, thereby enhancing the dealer's business and his image. So while able to deliver to the politician his safe seat, the gun could also serve as a handy item in the narcotics trade. The only problem was, who would provide or "bring in" the guns? And where, and how, would they be purchased? To answer these and other questions a more extensive discussion of the violent features of much of Jamaica's recent political culture is necessary, notably the aspect of what is often called "political victimization."

Simply put, political victimization means bestowing the largesse of government (public service employment, work contracts, housing, and so forth) on those who voted for a given political party in the most recent general election, and flagrantly denying it to those who did not. Playing the central roles here have been the country's two principal political parties, the Jamaica Labour Party (JLP) and the People's National Party (PNP). Both parties have historically found themselves in a fundamental dilemma: both have been forced to seek electoral support from among the poor, who have always constituted the most numerous sector of the voting population. But the demands from the poor confronting the victorious party have always outstripped the resources of government—hence the victimization of loyalists whose political party is out of office.

Nowhere has the practice of political victimization been more flagrant than in the *sufferah* communities of West Kingston and lower urban St. Andrew. Beginning in the late 1960s, under the rapaciousness of some of the countries' leading politicians, these communities were turned into what the late political sociologist Carl Stone calls "garrison constituencies"; that is, local seats of power, which, throughout the ceaseless years of eternity remain, and *must* remain in the control of one of the two political parties. This more often than not, is accomplished through thuggery, intimidation, vote fraud, and violence.[35] In these constituencies, a community's "top ranking" or most-feared gangster, its "don," becomes the conduit for the dispensation of party patronage. Eventually, the "top ranking" and their "rude bway" underlings assume local positions of power. Close links with the politicians afford the "top ranking" access to work contracts, police protection, and other favours. On the other hand, close links with the "top ranking" permit politicians to foment ferocious intraclass struggles which leave unchallenged a basic political-economic system that continues to reproduce poverty and deprivation.

The violent activity of the "top ranking" and their underlings first assumed a political character in the 1967 general elections, when both JLP and PNP candidates in West Kingston recruited gangs and street thugs to establish Party turf, or "safe seats." Violence and intimidation were used to ensure loyalty at the polls. It was, therefore, the country's leading politicians who brought in the guns and established the first contracts with international gun merchants.

Of course, it is nearly impossible to point to incontrovertible evidence linking any one politician to the wholesale illegal importation of guns into the country, but according to Michael Kaufman, "many Jamaicans believe that Mr. Seaga bears a major responsibility for introducing guns into Jamaican politics."[36] In addition, a wealth of information supporting the larger contention of a connection between drugs, guns, and politics is presented by Doris Kitson. She, too, contends that Seaga is to blame for introducing guns into partisan squabbles. She quotes the following from a *Covert Action* investigative report:

> On his [summer 1980] trip to the U.S., Seaga [at the time leader of the Opposition] 'predicted' more violence in store for Jamaica. Upon his return, his prediction was mirrored in further gunfighting, most of it coordinated and focussed. Gangs of youths who were known to have little money and no resources suddenly had vague 'jobs' getting $100 a week, motor-scooters, and a gun. . . . Some of the gang members, killed in shootouts, were discovered to be in possession of large amounts of cocaine. Indeed, eyewitnesses had often described the assailants as drug-crazed or 'zombie-like'. . . .[37]

Of the 800-odd murders reported for the island in 1980, most were attributed to political violence between the island's two warring political "tribes." More recently, the American news media ran two conspicuous stories linking the country's two top political leaders with known gangsters. In summer 1992, cable television's Cable News Network (CNN) did a story on the manufacture and sale of illegal U.S. passports, said to have been widespread in Jamaica among other places. Among other scandalous things, the story made much of a photograph of then recently retired Prime Minister and PNP President Michael Manley at a New York fundraiser. Mr. Manley was pictured in a lighthearted mood with a group of gang bangers wanted for murder in Jamaica.[38]

Earlier that same summer, National Public Radio's (NPR) "Morning Edition" did a major piece on similar gang ties to the JLP. Mr. Seaga and other top Party members, the story said, had attended the funeral earlier that year of one Lester Lloyd Koch, alias "Jim Brown," who was wanted in the United States on murder and narcotics charges. U.S. authorities suspected Koch of running the Jamaican end of a gun and cocaine-smuggling operation. He had also "ran" Seaga's parliamentary constituency.

So, at first, the guns served the specific partisan purpose of safe-seat-making and forging ties between the politician and the badman, but by the mid-1970s, their function was enlarged: they became essential items in the international traffic in illegal drugs. Before long, the island was literally overrun with M16s and Uzis, giving rise to the self-serving rumour—not entirely without some truth—that the Jamaican police were "outgunned" by the criminals. The politicians seemed as though they were about to be "consumed," and the political system subverted, by the "fire" *they* had started. The PNP government under Michael Manley, reacting (some say overreacting) to massive pressure to "get the guns off the street," passed a repressive Suppression of Crime Act in 1974 and instituted a controversial special "Gun Court."[39]

Manley and JLP leader Edward Seaga later got their leading "top ranking" to sign a "Peace Treaty," a move that only momentarily reduced street-level sales and distribution of the guns. Primarily because the drug traffickers and other thugs needed them, the guns had come to stay. Besides, the traffickers soon discovered that trading in both guns *and* drugs (sometimes one used in exchange for the other) was the more sophisticated entrepreneurial thing to do; it was a way of diversifying one's interest.

We should note, though, that on the matter of political violence, the society has come a long way from the dark 1980 election days. The death toll in the two subsequent recognized general elections (in February 1989 and March 1993) declined appreciably. Among other things accounting for an overall decline in election violence have been symbolic and generally extravagant ceremonial public signings of preelection "truces" (the equivalent of cease-fires) between the leaders of the two main rival political parties. Compared to the slaughter of 1980, during the 1993 campaign "only" fourteen politically motivated murders were reported, according to *The Washington Post*.[40] "There were reports of scattered shootouts in some poor, downtown areas of the capital, where violence traditionally has been worst. The Kingston hospital reported treating nine gunshot victims, including a policeman."[41]

Despite this optimistic report, many civic, business, and community leaders are not all that sanguine about the long-term prospects for the disappearance of political violence from the Jamaican crime scene. In an apparently well-received address following the PNP's rout of the JLP in the 1993 election, prominent business leader Dennis Lalor remarked that, "By all accounts, this election was perhaps the worst conducted—being firmly in the grip of gunmen and political activists, and in planning for the future, we must recognize that if democracy ever fails in this country, it will be because of that approach, rather than because of any desire to institute a military dictatorship."[42]

## Exportation of Criminal Elements

We now turn to two remaining questions:

- How did Jamaican crime, and crime networks, get exported into cities of the metropolitan countries, mainly the cities of the United States?
- What accounts for the return, or re-export back to Jamaica, of its criminal elements?

As was the case for trying to trace the specific ties between politics, thuggery, and the importation into the island of illegal guns, so, also, do we not have clear-cut answers to the two questions we are about to contemplate. These are just not the kind of things for which people leave paper trails or are willing to discuss—at least not for the record. By piecing together isolated bits of information, however, and by relying on insights gained from my participant observation, a plausible picture emerges regarding the export of Jamaican crime to the United States. I will come back later to the re-export of Jamaican criminal elements.

I posit three principal ongoing factors as responsible for the export of Jamaican crime into the cities of North America.

- First is the mysterious, typically illegal migration of known, senior "top rankings" to cities such as New York, Chicago, and Miami. This group has consisted mostly of men between the ages of thirty and forty whose criminal records are widely known in Jamaica. For the most part, they migrate to the United States by bypassing completely the American authorities, or they travel on forged passports and other travel documents.
- Second is the migration of a younger generation of "rude bways," primarily youths in their teens and early twenties who, while in Jamaica, may have had minor scrapes with the law. They would, however, blossom into full-fledged adult offenders in the United States. As youngsters in Jamaica, their upbringing on the streets of some of the island's toughest urban "jungles" would render them as fearsome as their more senior "top ranking" counterparts. Depending on type and quality of U.S. sponsorship, these youngsters would come to America on either temporary visas or as permanent, green-card-holding residents. After a few years' stay, some green card holders would (if their records were still clean) go on to gain naturalized U.S. citizenship status.
- Third is the integration of a subset of first-generation Jamaican youths into existing U.S.–based Jamaican crime and narcotics activity. Although American citizens by birth, these youngsters entire systems of identification and sense of cultural belonging are with the things and people belonging to "yard." Their individual

> identities and definitions of reality are shaped in a constant process of exchange and primary interactions with some of the more unsavory characters arriving from the home country, including associations with the "rude bways" coming up from the streets of Kingston. These contacts and cultural reinforcements often lead to gang recruitment.

Each of the three factors deserves closer scrutiny.

Returning to the matter of migration of known criminals, one vivid example helps make my point. In the 1970s, Bucky Marshall was a known PNP "top ranking." He was in his early thirties. Marshall and his JLP counterpart, Claudie Massop (also in his thirties), had for years led pitched PNP-JLP battles in the West Kingston ghettos. Both men had extensive criminal records. Marshall, in fact, had several murder raps against him. Politically related gang hostilities declined in Jamaica in 1978, when Marshall and Massop negotiated a truce and signed, in a much-ballyhooed public ceremony (witnessed by the country's top political and civic leadership), a "Peace Treaty." Only a few months after its signing, however, the "Peace Treaty" unraveled. "[G]un play had returned to West Kingston, and the police reported a slow re-emergence of gang warfare," write Stephens and Stephens.[43] Massop was subsequently killed in a hail of gunfire by the Jamaican police; and Marshall was killed in, of all places, New York!

The pressing question here is this: how did Massop, a known, if not necessarily a convicted, murderer get from Jamaica, "clean out of the country," to the United States? The answer is "connections." Along with all the other benefits—access to arms, cash, the good life—of dubious associations with "big time" politicians comes the prospect of being able to shuck it all and obtain travel documents to America, a feat that for most law-abiding Jamaicans is a formidable challenge. Clearly, the "right" telephone call to the "right" person can result in the relocation of even a feared gunman and/or drug trafficker to just about any place with which Jamaica has "good" diplomatic relations.[44] Once abroad, the "top ranking" merges into an existing criminal/drug network by, among other things, capitalizing on criminal contacts made while in Jamaica and/or cashing in on debts owed.

The second factor I suggest as responsible for the commission of crimes by Jamaicans in the United States relates to youngsters born in conditions of *sufferation in* Jamaica but who managed to migrate to America. To sustain themselves and their families, the mothers—and often enough the fathers—of these youngsters had to migrate. Mother would take a job in the rich white folks' homes out in places like Westchester County, New York, or Winnetka, Illinois. And father would leave to do itinerant farm work in Florida or Virginia. Or if father had not migrated, he might simply be "unavailable."

In some instances, both mother and father would emigrate together, and as a team they would work for some wealthy couple who at one time or another had come to Jamaica in search of "good" domestic help. Mother would work in the house, while father would tend the lawn or do the chauffering. In either case, children, some of them mere babies, would be left in Jamaica. If they were lucky, a grandparent or other extended family (often in a rural parish) would raise them; if not, as was all too often the case, nurturing and child care would be irregular, unordered, and dispersed.

Permanent separation between children and parents was never really intended. A time would come when parents and children—or at least mother and child—would be reunited; or so it was hoped. This would be done by saving enough money to allow a parent to either return home or "send" for the children, that is, bring them to America. More often than not, the dream of returning home—at least while the children are still young—would become ever more elusive. Thus, the more realistic alternative becomes sending for one's children.[45] But sending for offspring left in Jamaica, either to come up as visitors or permanent residents, is not easy for parents whose own immigration status in the United States is, at best, uncertain. It can, therefore, take years before parents and children are actually reunited in America.

For children without extended family nurturing in Jamaica, the years of separation would be difficult, tough ones. If the time was spent without stable nurturing in the shantytowns of Kingston, Spanish Town, or Montego Bay, the pressure toward the hustle of the street would be virtually unavoidable. A number of them would indeed succumb, although several more would *not*. But, typically, the years of unintended neglect and misery would drive many left-behind youths into street crime and various hustlings. The mere babies that parents had left in Jamaica a matter of a few short years earlier would grow into street-smart, tough little gang bangers. Some would grow into "rude bways." Because they were juveniles, however, they technically would have no criminal records, despite the seriousness of some of their misdeeds. Their parents, now straight with the American immigration authorities, could now successfully send for them. The youngsters would "land" on the streets of Brooklyn, Miami, Washington, D.C., Chicago, and Evanston (a Chicago suburb). They would come as the disenchanted, separated "children of Sisyphus." Several would be armed and extremely dangerous, if not with actual weapons (at least not yet), then certainly in mindset and temperament. They would tell mothers who had scrubbed white people's kitchen floors six and seven days a week to be able to send for them not to "lecture" them. Their manly pretentions would not, however, save them from being isolated from and further marginalized by a strange, unforgiving and foreign public-school system, whose administrators, counsellors, and teachers neither speak nor understand their Jamaican "language." It is from within this cohort of disaffected youthful immigrants that significant recruitment into American-based Jamaican crime networks takes place. Several of these networks would have international connections.

Jamaican criminal activities (especially those that are drug-related) thrive in the United States because of ongoing recruitment of a subsector of first-generation Jamaican-Americans, the "Jamericans." The most likely recruits are youngsters born in America to parents who never did quite manage to break out of domestic and other "unskilled" work, despite their untiring efforts at doing so. These families would be condemned to ghettoization, American style. The children would, therefore, come to face the same problems of economic marginality and a hostile criminal justice environment as their African-American counterparts.

In other words, the same structural forces within the American political economy and racial ordering which have over the years served to disproportionately incarcerate young American black men[46] would also serve, in the 1980s and 1990s, to destroy a sizeable segment of the population of first generation Jamaican-Americans. Their demise is often hastened by a murky twist: the strong admiration and cultural attachment that many tend to hold toward their "top ranking," "rude bway," and badmen brethren constantly arriving from "yard."[47] In all too many instances, it is this sanguinary group of incomers, with their tempestuous rage, dancehall pizazz, Jamicanized version of hip-hop, and a mash-dem-down "roots" culture, who provide definitive role models for many alienated, insecure youthful Jamaican-Americans, youths who are basically unsure of their "real" identity.

We turn, lastly, to the re-export, back to Jamaica, of those criminal elements of whom many in the Jamaican society may have thought the nation had managed to "cleanse" itself. Some 3,500 Jamaicans found guilty or suspected of criminal activity in the United States were forcibly returned to their island home between 1987 and the end of 1992. Over the course of those five years Jamaicans with a "questionable history" made up one-fifth of all U.S. deportees. Their return home was tied mostly to the United States "war on drugs" and to a lesser degree to an overburdened American criminal justice system.

Jamaicans in the United States were seen as one of the primary suppliers of illegal drugs into the American market when the Reagan administration began its highly touted "war on drugs," in the mid-1980s. Consistent with their ideology that social and economic problems get solved by regulating supply, not demand, the Reagan (and subsequently Bush) authorities embarked on a massive drive to expunge from the American society all (or as many as possible) narcotics-involved "aliens." Of the three variously predisposed Jamaican crime groups (i.e., those we just discussed) in America, two have always been particularly vulnerable to deportation orders—the senior "top rankings" who entered the United States via suspicious means and the younger "rude bways" who came in either as visitors or permanent residents.

U.S. Immigration and Naturalization law stipulates as grounds for automatic deportation any visitor or permanent resident convicted, in American courts, of a narcotics or narcotics-related charge. The law also allows for revocation of naturalized U.S. citizenship against anyone similarly convicted. (The same also goes for people wanted for war crimes.) Once citizenship is revoked, the next step is deportation to the person's country of origin. Typically, then, any Jamaican who is not a born American citizen lives under the constant threat of being sent back home. Faced in the late 1980s and early 1990s with burgeoning numbers of Jamaicans with vulnerable citizenship/immigrant statuses who were convicted on drug and drug-related charges, the easy way out for the American authorities was to send back home these least-protected Jamaicans. The others they would strip of their citizenship rights, then place them on the next aircraft bound for Kingston or Montego Bay. Both groups of criminal returnees, who had "refined" their expertise while in the United States, would add to the island's runaway crime problem.

To summarize, I have argued here that a pattern of dependent capitalist relations in Jamaica have served to produce a situation in which the scarcity of regular, socially acceptable work has condemned a substantial portion of the Jamaican population to an economically marginal existence. "Persistent poverty," to use George Beckford's apt phrase,[48] structural unemployment, and rural dispossession have given rise to acts of scuffling, petty hustling, street crime (often accompanied by extreme violence), and creation of an international drugs-and-guns network peopled by segments of a displaced working class who have historically found economic relief by migrating.

So from whence did we get such "bad" people? *We got them, and continue to get them, from the peculiar processes of our socioeconomic history and development.*

Before moving on to the all-important question of "What is to be done?" the next chapter takes a brief, passing look at what I think is a landmark study, one that drives home my central point about the critical causal relationship between social-economic conditions in Jamaica and the nation's high levels of crime, particularly violent crime.

# 3
# A Causal Relationship Reinforced

A study by sociologist Steven Messner, published in the *American Sociological Review*,[1] reinforces some of the things I tried to say in the preceding chapters about a history of social and economic dispossession contributing to high levels of crime and violence in the Jamaican society.

Messner examined for fifty-two countries, including Jamaica, the relationship between homicide or murder rates and a number of possible contributing factors, or independent variables. He used what might be considered "hard" 1980s' data, which he analyzed via rigorous, highly sophisticated statistical techniques. The independent or causal variables included income inequality, percentage of the population living in urban areas, population density, degree of political democracy, percentage of males fifteen to twenty-nine years old, and what he calls "level of economic discrimination."

He defined economic discrimination as "the deliberate, invidious exclusion of social groups from some desired economic goods or conditions . . . because of the groups' ascribed characteristics," including such characteristics as skin colour, family ties, regional identity, language differences (or inability to communicate in official language), religion, and social circumstance.

Data on each of these variables were reported for the fifty-two countries. The deciding factor in constructing an "economic discrimination index" was the percentage of people discriminated against. The percentages ranged from 0 percent discriminated against to a high of 95 percent discriminated against. Among the developing countries showing extremely low or 0 percent economic discrimination were Hong Kong, Costa Rica, Tanzania, and Zambia. In the case of Jamaica, the percentage of people discriminated against economically was a startling 77 percent. In fact, if we were to exclude the data for pre-independent Zimbabwe, which, as the author indicates, were "problematic," Jamaica would lead the list of fifty-two nations in level of economic discrimination—ahead of countries such as strife-torn Lebanon and most of Jamaica's Latin American and Caribbean neighbours.

The homicide rates per 100,000 population for each of the fifty-two nations were then statistically correlated with all twelve of the hypothesized contributing factors. The results showed that the countries with the highest levels of economic discrimination also experienced the highest levels of homicide. Furthermore, economic discrimination was *the* greatest single predictor of the number of homicides a country is likely to report in a single year. In other words, the greater the economic discrimination, the more homicides a country can expect. Jamaica's high rates of homicide—which from the mid 1970s to the end of the 1980s averaged between 17.0 and 22.0 per 100,000 population, among the highest in the region—were thus explained, to a high degree of statistical confidence, by the country's equally high level of economic discrimination.

Messner's study was not about Jamaica *per se*. Jamaica was included, or perhaps "thrown in," because it is one of a handful of developing countries which consistently provide relatively reliable data on social-indicator variables.

Based on the methodology employed and the extensive peer-review process I am sure this study underwent, I have no reason to doubt Professor Messner's findings—nor his conclusions. I accept them as facts. Whereas most academics will probably find the study merely "interesting" and well done, then shelve it in some out-of-the-way place, for Jamaicans everywhere the study intones a practical reality, a grim bottom line, which says: consolidated inequalities in the Jamaican society—with upwards of 77 percent of the Jamaican people being structurally locked out from the gains that the other 23 percent (or less) enjoy—produce pent-up aggression which manifests itself in diffuse hostility and random violence (a theme I shall return to in chapter four).

Having now, I think, fully made the case that crime in Jamaica is more than simply a police problem, I turn in the next two chapters to what has to be done in terms of (1) reconstructing the Jamaican society for the common good, and (2) reforming the way the nation does law enforcement and metes out punishment.

# 4
# What Is to Be Done to Achieve Greater Social Justice?

*A modern and humane political program will seek ways of dealing with the terrifying social fact that to survive in the modern world we must share in the making of each other's history because we share each other's moral responsibility.*

—Marcus G. Raskin

I tried to show in the preceding chapters that the workings of certain structural forces have produced, within Jamaica, not only an environment of anger and despair, but also an at-risk, crime-prone population which acts out that anger and despair. In this chapter and the next, I present, in light of the conclusions I have drawn about the social reality of Jamaican crime, what for the most part are admittedly ideological left-liberal solutions. I also think, though, that they are practical, realistic, and sensible.

The solutions I propose will, naturally, have very little to do with increased policing, *as we have come to know it*. Neither will I be calling for more wholesale incarceration of offenders—nor for more private security. Surely by now we should have learned that stronger burglar bars, more barbed wire, and more handguns all have the effect of making us only *feel* safe. They do nothing to change the motivation for and the logic of crime. As a matter of fact, available evidence indicates that the more guns people buy, presumably to protect themselves, the more they seem to end up being killed by them.[1]

Neither will any of my recommendations have anything to do with "beefing up" the Jamaican security forces—military and police—so that they can operate more "efficiently." The fact is, Jamaica has one of the best trained, most well-equipped police-military apparatuses in the entire English-speaking Caribbean. Tremendous inflows of U.S. dollars helped to reshape the country's security forces into a rough-and-ready fighting machine. The funds began pouring in with the U.S. Drug Enforcement Agency's (DEA) onslaught on the island's *ganja* growers in the mid 1970s. More funds came with President Ronald Reagan's launching of an Anti-Terrorism Assistance Program and a Security Assistance Program designed for a select group of Caribbean countries, with Jamaica, under the 1980s' strong pro-U.S. Seaga government, being the leading recipient. Jamaica's foray into Grenada, in October 1983, to help Mr. Reagan and the U.S. military "rescue" that country from communism was testament enough to Jamaican security forces' fighting capability. Jamaican law enforcement, inclusive of its police and army, are not, in other words, always "outgunned" by the criminals, the dark mutterings to the contrary notwithstanding.

Still, despite all their weaponry and overseas training, Jamaican law enforcement has not been measurably effective at reducing overall levels of crime. Crime still goes up—or certainly fluctuates, as we saw in chapter one—from year to year independent of police action. This has led, understandably, to rising levels of frustration within the police rank and file, resulting in the kind of police "excesses" (i.e., indiscriminate use of deadly force) that have been widely reported by international human rights organizations.[2] Finally, I am not going to recommend that the Jamaican society needs to deal more harshly with those whom its courts find guilty. Again, apart from a number of brutally repressive regimes in Latin America, Jamaica comes out ahead of nearly all other nearby countries at locking up its guilty. Furthermore, the rate at which the Jamaican government executes people is one that the rest of the civilized international community finds troubling.[3] Yet none of this has appreciably altered basic crime patterns, since overall crime rates remain unacceptably high. The society will, therefore, have to turn toward structural remedies for crime, toward addressing deep-rooted social forces that produce and reproduce motivated offenders, people who are not deterred by burglar bars, barbed wire, guard dogs, prisons, or the gallows.

At the core of the series of recommendations I will propose are two essential suppositions. The first is that creation of a social-economic system that can deliver greater social justice to all the Jamaican people is both a moral imperative and a recipe for *preventing* crime. The second is that proactive and imaginative strategies for enforcing the law and for punishing the guilty are not only hallmarks of a responsive and responsible society, they are also practical ways for *reducing* crime. In this chapter, I will focus primarily on the matter of social justice as it relates to crime; I shall then take up the issue of law enforcement and punishment in chapter five.

## A Dubious Development Road

My basic conclusion about the causes of high levels of street crime in Jamaica, and change in the patterns of those crimes, is that they are closely linked to the nation's larger crisis of economic production and system of social rewards. The upheavals that the society has undergone in recent years in the way it (re)produces and distributes goods, services, money, power, and social roles, including those based on class, race, and gender, have all contributed significantly, I am saying, to the country's crime problem. A fundamental solution, then, rests on taking a serious reassessment of the nation's political, social, and economic development process, and the changes in social dynamics that process has engendered.

The developmentalist road on which Jamaica has been traveling in the postwar years has produced little by way of productive employment and other entitlements of social justice. Quite the contrary is in fact the case, since the nation in which the present generation of Jamaicans live is one in which economic discrimination prevails (see chapter three), the criminalized are always the poor and the powerless (see chapter two), and the police, who by and large are unaccountable to the community they serve, fight crime by committing more crime, particularly against people defined as the least desirable.

The ultimate remedy for crime and violence, I submit, is building national ideological commitment toward implementing structural, democratic mechanisms capable of delivering greater social and economic justice to all the Jamaican people. These mechanisms should be able to intervene, through jobs and social-educational programmes, in lives that are at risk of becoming involved in crime.

Creating a society for the common good—where every woman and man can sit under and enjoy her and his own vine and fig tree—will not only reduce social pathologies such as crime, it will also reduce the need for large numbers of the Jamaican people to migrate for purely economic reasons. And intricately tied to the cultural habit of outmigration, I pointed out, is the export of Jamaican crime.

The underlying moral-ideological thrust of my solutions/recommendations is, therefore, aimed at changing the real-life, alienated, and deprived circumstances in which the vast majority of the Jamaican people (upwards of 77 percent) find themselves. But I also suggest some rather practical and implementable strategies. And as we examine closely these strategies, it should become apparent that no single one can in isolation be *the* preventive "cure" for crime. Each one, including those in the next chapter, will have to be acted on jointly, with each one serving to complement and reinforce every other one. Moreover, with only one or two exceptions, the recommendations and strategies I propose are for the long term. In neither social policy nor law enforcement are there quick-fix solutions to crime. Often required is whole societies turning several degrees in setting new agendas and priorities for the collective whole.

The specific social justice recommendations I will discuss in some detail can be categorized as follows.

*What is to be done to establish social justice?*

- Foster a development process that includes everyone.
  - Correct economic inequality.
  - Reinforce the right to development, including the right to an adequate education for everyone.
  - Reinforce the right to participate.

- Re-emphasize the primacy of the land.
- Implement measures for taking the pressure of economic "adjustment" off the poor.

*What is to be done to advance social justice once it has been initiated?*

- Create high-impact jobs for crime prevention.
- Develop a concept of community-service work.
- Strengthen educational, counseling, and outreach programmes for young people in trouble.
- Present alternate incentives to gang bangers.

## Foster a Development Process That Includes Everyone

In 1981, the International Commission of Jurists, under the auspices of the United Nations, held a conference on development, human rights, and the rule of law. Their published report emphasizes the linkage between the development process, social justice, and the reduction of crime.[4] I shall draw on some of the themes of that report in delineating my first "what is to be done" recommendation.

A development process that includes everyone means, first of all, political-ideological commitment to the notion that *all* of a nation's people have a right to development. This means, in operational terms, reduction of the social and economic inequalities that divide and separate people. It also means genuine democratic participation in the process of self-government. Let me elaborate.

### *Correct Economic Inequality*

Something we have not dealt with in any great depth so far is the extent to which relative deprivation has been responsible for Jamaica's crime problem, so let me do that briefly here.

My earlier research on crime in Jamaica also examined Jamaica's pattern of income distribution for the years 1950 through 1980. Much of the discussion that follows on economic equality in Jamaica is based on that work.[5] The data I gathered showed that from 1960 until 1974 the Jamaican economy achieved a relatively high rate of economic growth, with Gross Domestic Product (GDP) expanding at the rate of roughly 5 percent per year. But inequality remained severe, and even worsened, during each of those years. Little wonder that when the PNP came to power in 1972 they found popular support for the Party's wide-ranging programme of structural reforms, which it sought to implement under the banner of "democratic socialism." Real economic development in terms of improved productivity in agriculture, increased access to education, longer life expectancy, and an increasingly important role played by industry did take place throughout most of the 1960s. And from the late 1950s through the early 1970s real wages rose substantially.

However, while the nation's total national income (i.e., total monetary value of all final goods and services produced in the economy) increased by some 400 percent between 1960 and 1970, the already relatively small portion that went to the poorest households experienced further erosion over those same years. On the other hand, the percentage going to the wealthiest households was, as might be expected, significant—and increasingly so. The percentage of total national income going to the poorest households—which constituted roughly 45 percent of all households—was 4.4 percent in 1955; it declined steadily to under 2 percent by 1980, for an average annual rate of decline of 0.5 percent. The wealthiest households (about 4 percent of all households) were already receiving 30 percent of the national income in 1955; by the early 1980s, they were receiving close to twice that amount. All wage and salary earners, in fact, experienced relative income declines. In 1977, they shared 66 percent of national income; by 1990, they were sharing less than 50 percent.

The underlying explanation for this inequality is that Jamaica's industrialization programme has over the years relied on providing high profits for domestic and foreign investors.[6] So, by and large, Jamaica's pattern of development (especially in the 1960s) served essentially to build the country's national capitalist class, even though they remained an underdeveloped or perverted capitalist class, as is also true in other countries in the region, such as Mexico.[7] Thriving on protection and subsidies, Jamaica's capitalist class, like their Mexican counterparts, "learned that the path to profits lay more in making special arrangements with the state than in building the productive capacity of their enterprises."[8]

That aside, what is indisputably true for Jamaica is that although economic growth did occur, whole segments of the society were being systematically denied the prosperity and material happiness that a privileged few enjoyed, and that the gap between the haves and the have-nots has been widening almost daily in the last thirty or so years.[9] A situation of both absolute and, more important, relative poverty has prevailed.[10]

If Jamaicans are serious about reducing crime, the nation's gross levels of income/economic inequality will have to be drastically altered. "Around the world, at every level of economic development," writes criminologist Elliott Currie, "increasing equality goes hand in hand with lower risks of homicide."[11]

Not unlike the study reviewed in chapter three, in a careful analysis of murder rates in thirty-one countries, from poor ones in developing countries to advanced industrial societies, John and Valerie Braithwaite concluded that higher homicide rates were linked with several measures of economic inequality. The primary ones were (1) a broad gap between the rich and the average wage earner, (2) large disparities in income between workers in different sectors of industry, and (3) a low per capita consumption of protein—usually indicating a "wide gulf between the poor and the remainder of the population."[12] Using only slightly different measures, Steven Messner, in an earlier study than the one examined in chapter three, arrived at similar conclusions for thirty-nine capitalist-dominated countries that spanned the range of economic development. Income inequality explained, he discovered, a substantial 35 percent of the differences in homicide rates, even when several other factors—including population density, degree of urbanization, and level of economic development—were taken into account.[13] Similarly, a sizeable proportion of all murders committed in metropolitan America, the sociologists Judith and Peter Blau found, was related to income inequality—which, as the authors see it, "substantially raises" the rate at which people will kill and mete out other forms of seemingly gratuitous violence on others.[14]

In all the major studies done on the structural relationship between economic inequality and crime, the one constant is this: The societies that managed to escape extremes in criminal violence tend either to have highly developed public sectors with fairly generous systems of income support, relatively well-developed employment policies, and other cushions against the "forces of the market"; or, like Japan, they accomplish much the same ends through private institutions backed by an ethos of social obligation and mutual responsibility.

Many of the crimes that take place in Jamaica result from need, from widespread anger, and from resentment originating with the less-well-off members of the society. Resentment has a way of developing into acrimony and bitterness, and a general unfeeling attitude. What is to be done to correct Jamaica's own situation of severe economic inequality—which I am saying is also in part responsible for the country's disturbingly high levels of violent crime—is government implementing and more effectively enforcing wage policies that respect the labour of the poor and working class.

Furthermore, in those situations where international lending policies, or the "unleashing of the entrepreneurial spirit," result in the impoverishment of the already poor and dispossessed, both government and the private sector (including religious orders and organizations) will have to step in to succor the least able. They should do so through provision of meaningful subsidies and granting of other earned and unearned income credits. Yes, these will indeed *cost*!

### *Reinforce the Right to Development*

Although the specific problem of economic inequality does need remedying, development in its true, moral essence goes beyond income allocation or reallocation of benefits.

Development means securing an environment in which *all* of the people within a given polity can realize their fullest human potential. Every state has as its primary responsibility the promotion of the economic, social, and cultural development of its people, says the U.N. commission on crime and social justice. "To this end, each state has the right and the responsibility to . . . fully mobilize and use its resources, to implement progressive economic and social reforms . . . "[15]

A nation's true index of development, then, is the sum development of all its citizens. "Everyone has the right to social security and is entitled to realization . . . of the economic, social, educational and cultural rights indispensable for his personal development"; that is, the right to a "reasonable living standard, including adequate food, clothing and housing."[16] The underlying point is that social justice takes precedence over legal justice. The Jamaican government, whatever its partisan stripe, must therefore seek out ways and institute policies that will allow the full blossoming of the Jamaican people. This must be done especially for the nation's working-age population, who must be able to acquire the kind of educational and technical skills that are indispensable in the new globalized order. Development cannot be for some—for big capitalists, government officials, careerists, and the intelligentsia. It must be for all.

When people come to see that the realization of their basic worth is the only business of government, the meaning of society will take on new life. They will come to see society as something one builds, not something one destroys through crime and other antisocial activity. In other words, when the people whose labour the Jamaican society needs come to see that their well-being forms the basis of the nation's political belief system, its *weltanschauung*, they will not only steal, rob, maim, and murder less, they will also produce more and work harder—and longer.

### *Reinforce the Right to Participate*

The right to development becomes real only when people can participate fully in its unfolding and, ultimately, in its benefits. Citizens—all citizens—must be involved in the political dialogue over, among other things, the nature of government, the role of the state, organization of the means of production, management of scarce resources, school and educational reform, protection of the natural environment, and so on.

Participation in the nation's affairs means more than a five-minute formality, every four or five years, in the voting booth. What happens to and in the nation between general-election years is still everybody's business. During the "waiting period," issues still have to be resolved and decisions that affect the well-being of the entire nation have to be made. As things now stand, these decisions are made without the ongoing give and take of the people. Instead, they are made by a narrow political and business elite. True democracy requires that government consult continuously with the folks at the grass roots. The monopolistic control of state power by the country's two-party system distorts the idea of democracy. A more genuinely pluralistic system of governance is necessary if the Jamaican people are to be convinced that they have a real voice in the say-so of running their country. A governmental system that not only divides in order to rule, but then turns around and effectively excludes the people from participation, invites violent reprisals, some of which might be visited directly on government itself (as in organized insurrections and mass rebellions); others may take the form of loosely defined criminal activity.

What is to be done, therefore, is progressive communities within the larger society initiating strategies that will deepen the democratic process. The system I envision would be one characterized by government from the bottom up. Such a system would reduce the role of the professional politician and, ultimately, the level of dependence on the state. It would comprise a variety of movements and indigenous nongovernmental organizations (NGOs), a system of ordinary people participating as coequals in the business of government. This is nothing less than a concept of diverse, empowered people from different socioeconomic walks of life coming together to dialogue, debate, and arrive at mutually beneficial solutions—all done in the lively, not always orderly, process of direct democracy. In such a system, people would cease to be merely acted-upon objects who always seem to have decisions made for them. They would no longer be powerless supplicants to the state, to a political party, or to a Party boss. They would become, instead, subjects actively participating in "shaping their own destinies," in the terminology of Brazilian sociologist Paolo Freire.[17] Am I, then, calling for formation of a "serious" third, fourth, or fifth political party in Jamaica? More than that, I am calling for the formation of several alternate *movements* (not political "parties" in the conventional sense) to the two hegemonic party organizations that presently dominate the society. In a more decentralized, pluralistic environment, I can see where if one of Jamaica's two principal political parties is to govern, that party could conceivably be forced into entering coalitions with the people from below.

People's movements and NGOs do not have to grow into centralized, bureaucratized party apparatuses. They can remain strong, inner-directed movements yet be key players within the political-state structure. Solidarity groupings that are fully integrated into a system of political governance can give a new lease on life to an oppressed people.

Who knows, maybe if Jamaica's multitudes had a more direct role to play in the liberating exercise of governing themselves, they would not be so given to the alienating behaviour of flinging bottles at a musical legend, as they did at reggae singer Bunny Wailer at the 1990 Christmas concert held at the National Stadium, or of resorting to hideous incantations of "more slackness," as has been done at just about every mass musical event of the 1990s. What's more, when people come to see themselves as creative, ongoing participants in the political discourse over the shaping of their collective well-being, the alienation and powerlessness that breed violence, crime, and destruction will disappear. The need to take to the streets in an orgy of death and recrimination—or just to make sure *fi wi man* (or woman) "get in"—will be moot.

## Re-emphasize the Primacy of the Land

The incidence of Jamaican street crime (conventional and drug-related), I pointed out in chapter two, is intimately tied to the underproduction of jobs, especially long-term, meaningful jobs. But just how to generate enough jobs for an ever-expanding supply of youthful job seekers is the bottom-line issue confronting just about all developing societies.

The creation of a society that offers full employment—that is, job opportunities for everyone who wants to and is able to work—has to be the stated, committed, long-term goal of any political project with a serious desire to reduce crime. The evidence thus far on how well Jamaica has progressed toward full employment is not encouraging.

- First, the hoped-for massive job-creation possibilities of export-driven manufacturing concentrated in major urban areas of the island has been subjected to various fits and starts.
- Second, the desire to convert Jamaica into a prime regional commercial and financial showcase centre, offering lots of service-sector employment, is still a long way off, despite the occasional seemingly good prospects for this actually happening.
- Third, the tourist industry, with its few backward linkages into other areas of the local economy, most importantly agriculture, has proven more beneficial to a few well-capitalized local and international interests than to the mass of employable Jamaicans.
- And fourth, the bauxite industry, although providing government with reasonably steady supplies of foreign exchange in the form of tax levies, because of its capital-intensive (as opposed to labour-intensive) structure offers few new jobs. Bear in mind also that both tourism and bauxite suffer from cyclical problems and are both susceptible to prevailing worldwide market conditions.

In light of these facts, I see a renewed attention to an employment-centered approach to agriculture as the next best thing. I do so fully aware that the call for a re-emphasis on the "primacy of the land" (the onetime party line among development theorists) in a developing or underdeveloped economy is probably a dated idea. I am certainly not advocating a wholesale return to the canepiece and other primitive methods of sugar production. Sweeping changes in the world economy have long ago made the sugar estate, as Jamaicans and other West Indians have come to know it, a late-twentieth-century anachronism.

More appropriate for what has to be done are investment and serious long-term national commitment to land reform and agricultural production based on small- and intermediate-scale cooperative farming. These would be integrated into a system of agro-industry and farmers' markets. Government would provide start-up capital, organizational expertise, and infrastructural and market supports (storage, transportation and road systems, for example). Appropriate farming technologies which increase yields—and which, also, do not replace labour but complement and supplement it—would be continuously introduced. The key entity within this restructured system would be indigenous non-governmental organizations. They would be the catalyst—with government serving as facilitator and resource providers—for new projects. In this, one can only be encouraged by the PNP government's "Five-Year Development Plan, 1990–1995" for agriculture, in which, according to the Plan, "Research and extension programmes as well as new projects to be developed will focus on the need to assist farmers . . . to produce crops in which they have a comparative advantage."[18] Furthermore, according to the Plan, "It is the aim of the government to reduce the amount of idle land in the agricultural sector significantly, through the establishment of a Land Reform Programme."[19] We do, as of this writing have yet to see any serious move toward implementing this latter objective.

A structurally integrated system of agricultural production *with* decentralized sectors of local manufacturing (i.e., relocated outside the Kingston area), coupled with greater local value-added or forward links to tourism, would result in a significant flowering of more, and more viable, jobs.

Equally important for reducing crime would be the important spin-off benefit of an expanded agricultural system being able to regularize internal migration. Young men from the "country" areas would simply have less need to move to "town." Moreover, the stabilizing force of rural values—the high priorities placed on community, on sense of place, and on family, for instance—are generally more easily sustained within the indigenous social and cultural milieu afforded by this type of environment. The extent to which the entire Jamaican society is able to hang on to these values will strongly influence its level of crime.

People gainfully and productively employed within stable communities are, in the long run, the best guarantee a society has against crime and criminality.

## Implement Measures for Taking Pressure off the Poor

The World Bank and the International Monetary Fund (IMF) are the two international lending agencies to which most developing countries turn when they run into dire financial straits.

One of the IMF's "prescriptions" for breaking out of the cycle of debt and poverty is the elimination of government subsidies on most, if not all, consumer items.[20] The state should, in other words, remove itself from all forms of direct social-welfare type subsidies on items people need and consume the most. Government should then use the money saved to service existing debt.

The misery caused by this and other IMF-dictated policies of "structural adjustment" is a major contributor to political and social instability. But, in a world in which mainstream capitalist economic policy is the only game in town, the policies are defended as necessary to the long-run economic health of the countries involved. Political scientist John Peeler points out, however, that "this triumphal economics has its own myths that have pernicious effects."[21] The most pervasive, according to Peeler, is the myth of the "long run": the "idea that a market unfettered by political interference will, 'in the long run,' work to the benefit of all." It is assumed that those who suffer from competition will catch up in the long run. But there is no way "to confirm or deny this since the long run never seems to come."

A second myth, writes Peeler, is "that economics is a 'science.'" Few economists believe this. Nevertheless, "there is still a priestly aura about consultations with economists." He continues: "In today's complicated and rapidly changing world economy, economics is not a science with known, immutable laws; it is an arena for debate about choices."[22]

A third and final myth is that the best economic policy is one not contaminated by politics. The basic assumption of the IMF in its relations with developing countries is that it would be best for those who understand the "laws" of economics to carry them out, "minus ignorant politicians and citizens." The economists who work for the Fund presumably know what is good for a country and any political interference with the economic prescription is harmful.

But, Peeler correctly argues,

> In reality IMF prescriptions, like other economic policies, are inherently political. They represent choices about the distribution of resources. To minimize barriers to trade and government intervention is just as political as the idea of central planning.[23]

IMF policies of free trade, free market, pro-privatization, and government cutbacks are, indeed, the politically dominant ones in today's world. The sad truth is, though, wherever implemented their devastating effects have always fallen disproportionately harder on the poor and working class.

Removal of subsidies has meant, in Jamaica and other places, escalating costs for essential items such as food, clothing, housing, and health care. Prices of these items have been known to double, triple, and even quadruple during certain phases of an austerity programme, often provoking outbreaks of food riots and other acts of widespread violence, as occurred in relatively well-off Venezuela in 1989 and again in late 1992. When, in Jamaica, people who earn only marginal or subsistence wages—or no wages at all—are faced with daily increases in the price of bread, milk, meat, infant formulas, and medication, with no help coming from government, church, or other private agencies, just what are they supposed to do if they are to sustain themselves? Some may indeed turn to "The Lord." The more frustrated, who simply *caan tek no more* (as expressed in one of the era's graffiti), will explode in anger; others will prey on the seemingly better-off folks in the society—as well as on fellow *sufferahs*. "Outbursts" and violent property-related street crimes are, I am saying, one set of consequences of stringently enforced IMF rules and policies.

A policy of cutbacks that has the strongest impact on the poor and the working class is not only an unjust social policy, it is also inherently counterproductive, since it can eventually retard development. Increase in crimes committed out of need is an additional outcome.

What is to be done under conditions of unavoidable international lending strictures is that government must, first and foremost, focus more directly its austerity efforts at trimming unproductive jobs in the state sector, then retrain laid off workers. Next it will have to inaugurate a policy of discriminate subsidy removal. Poor and working-class people would continue to benefit from direct subsidies on essential items, while the well-to-do and the better-off segments of the society would not. Only after the poor have been given a chance to participate positively in the economic activity of the nation should they be expected to "pay" their fair share.

Lest this recommendation be misconstrued as a call for populist redistributionism in favour of the poor majority, let me stress that any policy of protecting the poor without adequate regard for the conditions for expanding production is doomed to failure. So in conjunction with a policy of directed subsidization, I am calling for creation of genuinely productive enterprises, which may indeed require various tax incentives to business investors. But accompanying creation of these enterprises should be built-in emphases on training and assisting young people to acquire modern work-related skills. The enterprises should, whenever possible, be targeted toward the nation's most truly disadvantaged communities, specifically communities experiencing rapid growth rates in the size of their youthful at-risk population. If necessary, borrow to fund them or to offset their cost (in, say, lost taxes) to government. The returns will pay off in the long run, since, as the Japanese and others have shown, investing in building a highly motivated and productive work force is the surest means toward accumulating real national wealth.

## Create High-Impact Jobs for Crime Prevention

Mere mention of impact jobs—as distinct from permanent or long-term jobs—for the chronically unemployed and underemployed is typically met with cynicism, if not outright laughter, as Jamaicans recall the "failed" high-impact "crash work" programmes initiated by the "democratic socialist" regime of the PNP in the 1970s.

In and of itself, the idea of putting idle hands to work on short-term, albeit make-work, projects can hardly be considered a bad objective. Toward the end of the sixteenth century, Richard Hakluyt depicted the ominous consequences of England's widespread unemployment. "For all the statutes that hitherto can be devised," he wrote, "and the sharp execution of the same in punishing idle and lazy persons for want of sufficient occasion of honest employment," it had proven impossible to

> deliver our Commonwealth from multitudes of loiterers and idle vagabonds, which, having no way to be set on work . . . often fall to pilfering and thieving and other lewdness, whereby all the prisons of the land are daily pestered and stuffed full of them, where either they pitifully pine away, or else at length are miserably hanged, even twenty at a clap out of some jail.[24]

The same problem worried American observers three centuries later. In 1878, the economist Carroll D. Wright, Massachusetts Commissioner of Statistics, noted that more than 67 percent of convicts in that state were recorded as "having had no occupation." Of 220 men sentenced to prison one year, "147 were without a trade or any regular means of earning a living." Wright warned of the disquieting implications of this for the "reform" of prisoners:

> Will these men serve their time, and be discharged in their present unfit state to battle with the world? They may go out into society again resolved to do right; but without a reliable means of support they are ill-prepared to meet the adversities of hard times, or the temptation to gain by crime what they do not know how to obtain by honest labor.[25]

The connection between crime and the lack of any regular means of earning a living has changed little since Wright's time, or even Hakluyt's. As I pointed out earlier, upwards of 70 percent of Jamaica's inmate population were not working either full or part time in the months prior to their (re)arrest and subsequent (re)incarceration.

Research in the United States suggests that unemployment is one of the variables found most often among the already "hardened" within prison populations. It is also strongly associated with *high-rate* offenders—that is, offenders who are disproportionately responsible for a significant number of all serious crimes.

These findings are no surprise. They fit our common-sense understanding of who goes to prison, and they are compatible with a broad range of theories of crime, including the economic or "rational-choice" approach favoured by many conservative thinkers. In a society in which work is the indispensable key to most things—material and otherwise—that our culture considers worth having, it's easy to see why those without work might try other, less legitimate ways to get them. And since work is also one of the most important ways individuals become integrated into a larger community, it isn't surprising that those excluded from the world of work will be held less tightly by the bonds that keep a society together. On the face of it, as I indicated under the recommendation for re-emphasizing agriculture, the appropriate response seems fairly cut and dried: if we want to lower the crime rate once and for all, we will have to do a better job of providing access to work—especially for young males in the largest urban areas, notably the Kingston Corporate Area. We will have to give them a stake in conformity.

The PNP's "crash work" programme had as its goal not only the provision of income to a disaffected and "crime-prone" sector of the urban population; its intent was also to connect the untrained to the disciplined world of work. Three things, it seems to me, went wrong with the programme. First, it involved spending enormous amounts of scarce public dollars; second, the jobs had overtones of political patronage; and third, the jobs were seen as essentially unproductive make-work which had no discernible connection or relationship to private means of production.

I do maintain, however, that implementation of some type of emergency work programmes, particularly in the more blighted areas of, say, downtown Kingston, are again necessary if we hope to really do anything about reducing crime. This time around, efforts should be made to eliminate the defects of the 1970s' programme by (1) removing them as far as possible from the politicians and the public payroll, leaving their management and implementation to community (including church) groups and NGOs; (2) involving in cooperative (as opposed to superordinate) ways the private business sector and private philanthropic organizations, both local and overseas; and (3) building in a quality component to the work enterprise, so that work products do, in fact, meet genuine social needs.

And just what kind of work enterprises might these be? They could include minimum-wage job programmes for razing derelict buildings in slum areas, using hammers and chisels, not bulldozers and wrecking balls. Then with the assistance of international community-assistance agencies—such as "Habitat for Humanity" (in which former President Carter is actively involved) or even the about-to-be-refocussed (under the Clinton administration) U.S. Agency for International Development (USAID)—and generous tax write-off/tax-credit funds donated by wealthy Jamaicans, several urban youths could be involved in building low-cost housing for other deprived urban dwellers.

Along these lines, projected plans for the restoration of downtown Kingston, under the Kingston Restoration Company (KRC) should, as a must, aim for maximum work opportunities for chronically unemployed and underemployed area youngsters. The planned development calls for, according to the KRC's Annual Report, improving access to the old Coronation Market, creation of a new marketplace, expansion of bus terminals, relocation of the craft market, and upgrading of the road network. Also in the plan is call for the renovation of derelict warehouses and other buildings, which will be converted into shops and "dwelling places."[26] No more useful purpose of private sector and USAID funds can be served than a venture of this sort, which would not only give needed improvement to one of the Caribbean's truly great cities, but also provide youngsters with an income and equip them with essential work skills.

The above are only a couple of examples of high-impact job creation that could serve as prevention to crime. With a little thought and imagination, others—such as, for example, sanitation and environmental projects (such as recycling), cooperative broiler farming, cultivating food crops on unused urban plots—could be added *ad infinitum*. My emphasis is on creating a variety of small, urban-based for-profit (or at least income-producing) projects that can involve and productively occupy hands that might otherwise turn to crime. The projects would require relatively small amounts of public funds, if any. Small innovative nongovernmental associations such as the Rosemary Development Fund, in downtown Kingston, could be one source of funding. The Fund gets people to pool a set amount of savings (based on the old practice of "partner"), which it then loans to others to start little businesses. Another funding source for essentially *grass-roots-based and grass-roots-initiated* crime-prevention projects should be the government-backed Micro Investment Development Agency (MIDA), which is geared to developing the microbusiness sector. Moreover, I would argue for diverting a portion of the funds the society currently spends on traditional law enforcement, public and private, into this sort of activity. No one, I should hope, would argue with the notion that an ounce of prevention is worth a pound of cure.

## Develop a Concept of Community-Service Work

I mentioned in the prologue that Jamaicans might consider adapting, or even borrowing wholesale, some of the more successful crime and delinquency prevention strategies that are presently being applied in parts of the United States.

One such strategy is a unique community-service programme in Boston, Massachusetts, called City Year. The programme places teams of young people, age seventeen to twenty-three, from different cultural and economic backgrounds, in community-service work for nine months. Participants receive a 100-dollar weekly stipend and a 5,000-dollar grant upon completion of the programme. The youngsters, who might be recent high school graduates, college graduates, or students studying to pass their high school equivalency tests, engage in all sorts of community work—organizing recreational programmes for senior citizens, restoring playgrounds and parks, repairing and painting shelters for the homeless, and serving as teachers' aides in Boston's city schools. The idea is to get young people more involved in community work while encouraging a spirit of teamwork, racial harmony, and social awareness.

The programme's co-director, Michael Brown, said in an interview in a January 1993 issue of *The Christian Science Monitor* that one of the most valuable benefits for these young people is the experience of rubbing elbows with others who come from a variety of backgrounds—from young people who have joined gangs to young people who have graduated from private prep schools.[27]

Each morning at 8:30, rain or shine, all 220 participants gather at Boston City Hall to do calisthenics. The group then splits into teams of ten members, each to work on community projects throughout the city. On Fridays, they take a break from their chores for "enrichment day," which includes workshops on racism, sexism, violence, drugs, and other issues. Co-director Brown says the programme helps young people build confidence in themselves through service to others. In high schools, team members work on internships that include helping kids with homework, indoor games, and art projects.

In a way, the goals and objectives of City Year are similar to those of President Bill Clinton's proposed national Youth Service Program—an idea that the PNP government of the 1970s had briefly toyed with. National service, or the idea of young people spending a year or two working for their community in exchange for government grants or a university education, is one that should certainly be seriously contemplated for Jamaica. Bringing together young Jamaicans from diverse cultural, economic, and, yes, "racial" backgrounds in a project of national uplift would (1) give ghetto youths an opportunity for meaningful social interaction with other youngsters considered fitting role models, thereby diverting potentially at-risk youngsters from a life of crime and waste, and (2) promote widespread appreciation for the values attached to service, volunteerism, and a communitarian spirit of egalitarianism, sharing, respect, and working together for the common good.

## Strengthen Educational, Counseling, and Outreach Programmes for Young People in Trouble

In Oakland, California, an innovative programme brings together parents and teenage offenders for intensive counseling in an effort to stem increasingly serious juvenile crime.

Rather than putting participating twelve- to fifteen-year-olds accused of burglary, theft, and similar crimes in jail or on probation, the Oakland court system diverts them into Project Re-Connect, a youth outreach programme where they and a parent or responsible adult go through eight weeks of counseling. At the end of the eight weeks, each offender must enroll for another year with a community programme such as Big Brothers/Big Sisters. Besides providing counseling, Project Re-Connect staff members also visit homes, investigate conditions faced by siblings, and recommend intervention.

The programme could become a national model for the entire United States. "If we're successful," said project co-founder John Burks in an interview in an April 1993 edition of *The Christian Science Monitor*, "the program will help young people before they become hardened criminals. It will 'wipe the slate clean,' and allow them to get on with their lives."[28]

Another programme, Youth Build USA, emphasizes "mental-toughness" orientation sessions for young people having trouble in school and with the law. In each two-week session, youths in the programme (age sixteen to twenty-five) prepare themselves mentally and physically for the "hard" work ahead. They learn how to apply for a driver's license, open a bank account, and get a library card, among other things. But they also spend time outdoors sawing boards, climbing ladders, and banging nails as they help rebuild shelters for homeless people. And, in alternating weeks, they go inside a classroom, where they take notes, study, and prepare for their high school equivalency test.

The idea of the programme is to give disadvantaged, undereducated youths a second chance in life. Says its president, Dorothy Stoneman: "On balance, you join a community, you're challenged to become a leader. You get a chance to go back to school, develop a skill and a good-paying career, serve the community by building housing, and be a part of a positive peer group."[29]

These programmes seem feasible for Jamaica. They two are geared specifically toward youngsters actually already in trouble with the law, or they are at the brink of getting there.

Mention of these programmes is not, of course, intended to undermine similar excellent outreach efforts being made *in* Jamaica. For example, the Alpha Boys School and Band, under the dedicated leadership of Roman Catholic nuns, has for over 100 years "given love and security of a home" to many troubled Kingston youngsters, "boys from what is politely called difficult social circumstances," notes writer Dermot Hussey.[30] The youngsters, many of them barely in their teens, come to Alpha as runaways or after stints in petty crime. "Often abandoned, they arrive at Alpha seeking care and protection, and are taught useful trades of printing and book binding, cabinet-making and in times past, shoemaking, tilemaking, blockmaking and pottery. It's music, however, that's been the trick of the trades, and its subsequent skill has made Alpha Boys School and Band an unparalleled Jamaican and Caribbean experience."[31]

Youngsters learn at Alpha to channel their frustrations into music. And so over the years the list of legendary local musicians to have come out of Alpha has "not only been impressive, but seemingly endless": Leslie Thompson, Bertie King, Dizzy Reece, Joe Harriott, Harold McNair, Wilton Gaynair, Tommy McCook, Don Drummond, Rico Rodriquez, Eddy Thornton, Cedric Brooks, Tony Gregory, Leroy Smart.

Then only recently I was introduced to another local outreach concept, called the National Youth Camp (NYC)–Jamaica. Its organizers engage youngsters in ongoing camp and counseling activities, with the objective of providing them with "cultural and extra-academic study . . . through which they may develop a better understanding of themselves and each other, a greater appreciation of their culture and a clearer image of their goals, and their roles in today's society."[32] A "Personal Development" component of NYC "is designed for young people who are serious about their future, " highlighting for them options available after high school and college.

These and other similar outreach programmes will have to be strengthened if the Jamaican society ever hopes to rescue itself from the damnation of more crime and save the lives of so many of its children from perpetual degradation. Church groups and other nongovernmental agencies which regularly conduct things such as camping experiences for *their* youngsters will have to expand their efforts, and perhaps their theology, to reach, connect, and include other youngsters—youngsters not quite so privileged, youngsters at drift, youngsters in trouble. The underlying point is that one of the ways in which a society can reduce its crime problem is by communities of solidarity (not exclusively, I emphasize, outside do-gooders or the state) intervening, as early as possible, in the lives of would-be long-term offenders.

## Present Alternate Incentives to Gang Bangers

In any number of instances, crime in Jamaica, particularly politically motivated and drug-related crimes, have involved "natural" leaders who were for the most part raised behind Kingston's ghetto walls.

Organized criminal and drug gangs—many of them with known connections to the island's two main rival political parties (see chapter two)—are continuously being formed and re-formed under the leadership of these intelligent, bright young men known as the communities' "top rankings." They are young men with considerable managerial, organizational, and motivational talents and skills. Within the underworld of crime and illegality to which they see themselves—sometimes justifiably—as condemned, they are people with both brains and brawn; they are entrepreneurs who, in the course of their brief lifetimes, acquire various money-making "skills"; they respect discipline and authority, albeit the authority of the gun; they are fiercely competitive and daring; and they know how to wield power and influence. Just ask any local, urban-based politician if this is not so.

What if these enormous talents were transformed into routine engagement in *legal* activities? With a little imagination and a lot less narrow partisan self-interest, the energies of many future natural ghetto leaders can be directed away from a life of meaningless violence and hustling into positive community uplift and self-help. All that has to be done is to find ways for developing a new or alternate system of incentives for the upcoming generation of potentially at-risk youngsters. If one of the cogent things that motivates the gang leader is quest for recognition, status, and power—as some criminologists believe[33]—then mainstream society would do well to re-concentrate its efforts toward finding means through which the driving ambition of naturally adventuresome youths can be channeled into a host of alternate activities. They should be challenged, for example, to sit on and exercise leadership roles on local school boards and/or councils, to participate and lead out in NGOs, to become block captains and sports and recreational leaders, and to work creatively with the police in building neighbourhood trust and co-operation (next chapter).

For the more immediate problem of what is to be done with the gang bangers and "top rankings" we already have, they can, and should, be given incentives to act positively. Make them captains of work and community projects that are removed from Party politics. They will, I truly believe, apply to them the same level of zeal, energy, commitment and hard work that they bring to gangsterism. Admittedly, that's some kind of faith in a supposed basic goodness of humankind; but it's a faith worth risking one's reputation on.

# 5
# What Is to Be Done About Law Enforcement and Punishment?

*Happy are those few nations that have not waited for the slow succession of coincidence and human vicissitude to force some little turn for the better after the limit of evil has been reached, but have facilitated the intermediate progress by means of good laws.*
—Cesare Beccaria

Common sense and intellectual honesty must go hand in hand with any serious analysis of crime and crime control. Even if Jamaicans were to construct the perfectly just society—that is, one along the lines suggested in the previous chapter—we would still, more than likely, have *some* crime. Thus, law enforcement and punishment, and a system of criminal justice that embraces both, will always be with us. And the politicians, so long as there are politicians, will continue to make laws designed for punishment, which others must enforce.

What kind of criminal laws a society makes, and how it chooses to interpret and enforce those laws, will largely shape that society's definitions of crime and, more important, determine how it will deal with criminal occurrences. Societal reactions to crime in the way criminal laws are made, interpreted, and enforced often bear equal responsibility for the perpetuation and increase in crime as do the pressures of social and economic disenfranchisement. So I will recommend in this chapter the kind of imaginative approaches to the law, to law enforcement, and to the idea of punishment that are likely to reduce the incidence of street crime *while we are trying to construct a more just society.*

What is to be done is, first, ensure that our concern with the control of crime does not become the basis for militarization of the society. Next, we need to institute a law-enforcement process that is more proactive than reactive, and which, also, allows for ongoing community inputs and control. Then we need to think through ways, make laws, and set policies that are aimed at rehabilitating and reconstructing lives that have been distorted and deformed by their resort to crime—to find ways, in other words, to integrate otherwise wasted and nonproductive young men and, increasingly, young women into the society of which they are in theory a part. Lastly, and perhaps intuitively counter to the Jamaican psyche, Jamaica will have to abolish its cruel and barbaric death penalty. The practice of hanging people by the neck until they are dead serves only to perpetuate an insistent cycle of violence.

So the recommendations I will discuss read as follows:

- Cut back the military and reallocate resources to the police.
- Apply the law equally.
- Build in community policing.
- Weed out and punish rogue cops.
- Change the way we punish.
- Reinforce drug-demand reduction.
- Place greater emphasis on basic skills and education in prisons.
- Strengthen prison industries.
- Deal creatively and constructively with prison overcrowding.
- Reshape popular attitudes toward the guilty.
- Abolish the death penalty.

## Cut Back the Military

Insertion of the Jamaican military into controlling crime and "disorder" goes back to the mid to late 1960s. The period's ruling political regime had convinced us then that numerous black nationalist and Rastafarian-inspired uprisings had possible "outside" influences and that Rastafarians, therefore, constituted a threat to the nation's security and newly won independence. This was the kind of threat, we were told, the military was most equipped—and constitutionally delegated—to handle. So we watched, often in dismay, as battalions of army boys, bayonets drawn, marched into and ransacked areas of the Kingston ghetto to quell "disturbance" after "disturbance." Increasingly since then, governments of both the JLP and the PNP have come to rely on the military as *the* effective arm of a visionless crime-control strategy.

Given the persistence of street crime, despite regular army crackdowns on the entire civilian population, I call for a rethinking of the overall role and function of the military in a democratic Jamaica. Do we, in the first place, really need a standing 3,000-person military force in Jamaica? And is use of the military to "fight" conventional crime in the civil society an acceptable practice?

Costa Rica, situated just on the other side of the Caribbean Sea from Jamaica, with a population larger than Jamaica's, has no standing military. For this and other reasons, Costa Rica is often regarded as the most democratic and most enlightened nation in all Latin America. One important outcome of Costa Rica's instructive approach to self-governing democracy is its much lower rate of crime, particularly violent crime. In

1980, for example, when Jamaica reported some 900 homicides,[1] Costa Rica reported 134, for a homicide rate of 5.9 per 100,000 population[2] compared to Jamaica's 50.1.[3]

Many years ago, the Costa Rican people discovered that none of their neighbours had, nor were they likely to have, any serious designs on their sovereignty or territory. They found out, furthermore, that the best guarantee a society is likely to have against threats and subversions from within was to (1) allow for continuous democratic participation in the affairs of the country and (2) make life more livable for all of the nation's people. It should come as no surprise, therefore, that Costa Rica was one of the countries in which sociologist Steven Messner (whose work was discussed in chapter three) found the least economic discrimination and, consequently, a low rate of homicide.[4]

The capacity to repel, by overwhelming force, any external threat to the security and sovereignty of a nation is, arguably, the *only* justifiable reason for maintaining a standing military. Just who or what country, pray tell, has designs on or is likely to attack, or invade, Jamaica? Haiti maybe? At least in the overblown cold-war years, someone might have listened (as the American CIA did) if we had said "the Cubans are coming," but now, with Cuban communism reduced to ox-drawn plows, what other nation is Jamaica protecting its borders from? But, after thirty-odd years of ceremonial displays, symbolic reassurance, and scores of successful military careers, any call to reassign our men in green to providing us with, say, a better-run post office or electrical power system is not likely to be treated seriously. The Newcastle and South Camp Road facilities, I guess, are here to stay. This is not to say that there aren't a few important jobs the Jamaican army in particular has, in the past, proven itself highly effective and efficient at performing—for example the assistance it has given to the civilian authorities in times of national disasters, plus its potential for providing "boot camp" experience as part of a larger rehabilitation strategy (discussed later).

We should, nonetheless, contemplate reductions in the amount of money the nation spends on the military. A force of 3,000 sitting in their barracks polishing their rifles while waiting for imagined enemies seems an enormous waste of scarce resources and valuable work skills. Although we may need the Coast Guard for "defence" against narcotics "invaders," we certainly do not need the offensive capability of an Air Wing.

That aside, placing greater reliance and emphasis on an expanded role for the military in protecting the society from street crime is an absolutely misguided notion. By its very nature and by the essentialist task it is expected to perform, the military is, and some would say *has to be*, antidemocratic and authoritarian. It is not subject to the changing circumstances, needs, value priorities, and popular discourse of civil society. The problem and root causes of crime are, if nothing else, complex and basically ideological. Its solution and control must, therefore, reside within those political institutions that are immediately accessible to the popular will—such as national and local legislatures and the local or town police. Aside from quelling clear and unambiguous acts of internal destabilization of legitimate, politically constituted civil authority (which is generally *not* true of most street crimes), the military has no business policing civil society. Thus, any structural "merging" of the functions of the military with the police would be not only unenlightened and backward; it would be inherently counter-democratic.

What is to be done is reduce the role of the military in crime control and drastically cut back on the money spent building it up, then redirect those dollars into hiring more police officers, providing them with training that is oriented toward bold, imaginative police methods. I am thinking in particular of a type of policing which embraces and encourages broad grass-roots participation. An educated police officer core will indeed come to see that popular participation in, and control of, the agencies of law enforcement are not only rights of citizens, they can also be useful strategies for reducing the incidence of crime.

## Apply the Law Equally

My focus in this book has been on the problem of street crime, leaving out, for the most part, official and so-called "white collar" crimes. I did so primarily because one can take on only so much in one book—not because they are any less important or any less dangerous (although they might be less frightening) to the well-being of the society. If, however, we expect to win in the battle against street crime, a more even application of the law will have to be developed.

In Jamaica as, of course, anywhere else, the law does not apply to everyone. An entrenched system of graft and cronyism (arguably no worse than in any developing country, or in Chicago) ensures that certain people, no matter what the nature of their offence, outside of maybe murder, never have to face the proverbial bar of justice.

The statistics on Jamaica's criminal population do show that the society readily criminalizes the misdeeds of the poor—especially the black poor—while ignoring the corporate and official wrongdoings of the powerful and wealthy. This is no way to generate universal respect for law and order.

We need a renewed determination, at all levels of the society, to apply the law evenly to *all* violators—not just to the street hoodlum, but to unscrupulous landlords, thieving businessmen, union-busting companies, tax cheaters, and government officials who steal, and waste, the people's money.

## Build in Community Policing

One of the things we should have done in 1962 when we asked the British to take leave of us was to insist that they take with them the idea of the police as paramilitary enforcers. Nothing has generated more tension, more disrespect, and more hostility between the police and the people they are supposed to serve than the notion that the police exist as "something" outside of and apart from the communities they are supposed to serve.

The image aspired to by many of the cops in today's Jamaica is of a mean, deadly crime fighter, a crusading, tough *hombre* who is here to cure a disease and to rid society of its scum. His skills were acquired and fine-tuned in the University of Hard Knocks; he has the stripes, as well as the notches on his gun, to prove it. Many Jamaican cops, I have found, see themselves in precisely those terms. At best, what the nation gets from this warlike self-definition is police brass making decisions about "what we are going to do about crime" over cocktails and expensive hotel dinners; at worst, it's police cowboys riding roughshod over citizens.

What is to be done is that we change the outsider conception of the police. Doing so would signal greater commitment to a democracy of law enforcement; it would also result in more effective policing. What is definitely not called for here is simply a matter of relying more on occasional outside citizen review boards or panels. Rather, I am advocating a transformation from the closed, strictly internal, paramilitary, top-down command-and-control structure of the police apparatus. The entire police organization must not only be opened up to citizen inputs, but it must also come under complete community control. Not only should the police hear directly from citizen groups about a community's specific needs, but also directives for type of police action should come from them. Groups of common, ordinary, everyday citizens should have an institutionalized role to play in the selection of the nation's Commissioner of Police. Candidates should be required to meet, dialogue, and debate with such groups.

This kind of reorientation at the top must then be supplemented by change at the ground-level, meaning, implementation of a new style of beat policing. Policing will no longer be driven purely by response to crime incidents but by ongoing cooperative relationships between residents and the police. I am, in other words, calling for a type of community-oriented policing that is presently being tried, with much success and community approval, here and in Chicago. What exactly is community policing?

Simply put, community or neighbourhood policing includes all efforts by the police and the community to work in partnership to mobilize, organize, and help empower residents to create crime-free communities.

As put by two of its most ardent proponents, criminologists Robert Trojanowicz and Bonnie Bucqueroux, "Community Policing is both a philosophy and an organizational strategy that allows the police and community residents to work closely together in new ways to solve the problems of crime, fear of crime, physical and social disorder, and neighborhood decay." The philosophy of community policing, they say, "rests on the belief that law-abiding people in the community deserve input into the police process, in exchange for their participation and support. It also rests on the belief that solutions to contemporary community problems demand freeing both the people and the police to explore creative, new ways to address neighbourhood concerns beyond a narrow focus on individual crime incidents."[5]

Trojanowicz and Bucqueroux go on to delineate a set of "principles" for community policing in the American urban setting. Eight of them seem especially relevant for Jamaica; they could, if given the will, be implemented in just about any Jamaican municipality. Those principles follow.

1. To implement true Community Policing, police departments must . . . create and develop a new breed of line officer, the Community Policing Officer [CPO], who acts as the direct link between the police and people in the community. As the department's community outreach specialists, CPOs must be freed from the isolation of the patrol car and the demands of the police radio, so that they can maintain daily, direct, face-to-face contact with the people they serve in a clearly defined beat area.
2. The CPO's broad role demands continuous, sustained contact with law-abiding people in the community, so that together they can explore creative new solutions to local concerns involving crime, fear of crime, disorder, and decay, with private citizens serving as unpaid volunteers. As full-fledged law enforcement officers, CPOs respond to calls for service and make arrests, but they also go beyond this narrow focus to develop and monitor broad-based, long-term initiatives that can involve community residents in efforts to improve the overall quality of life in the area over time. As the community's ombudsman, CPOs also link individuals and groups in the community to the public and private agencies that offer help.
3. Community Policing implies a new contract between the police and the citizens it serves, one that offers the hope of overcoming widespread apathy, at the same time that it restrains any impulse to vigilantism. This new relationship, based on mutual trust, also suggests that the police serve as a catalyst, challenging people to accept their share of the responsibility for solving their own individual problems, as well as their share of the responsibility

for the overall quality of life in the community. The shift to Community Policing also means a slower response time for non-emergency calls and that citizens themselves will be asked to handle more of their minor concerns, but in exchange this will free the department to work with people on developing long-term solutions for pressing community concerns.

4. Community Policing adds a vital proactive element to the traditional reactive role of the police, resulting in full-spectrum police service. As the only agency of social control open 24 hours a day, seven days a week, the police must maintain the ability to respond to immediate crises and crime incidents, but Community Policing broadens the police role so that they can have a greater impact on making changes today that hold promise of making communities safer and more attractive places to live tomorrow.
5. Community Policing stresses exploring new ways to protect and enhance the lives of those who are most vulnerable—juveniles, the elderly, . . . the poor, the disabled, the homeless. It both assimilates and broadens the scope of previous outreach efforts, such as Crime Prevention and Police/Community Relations units, by involving the entire department in efforts to prevent and control crime in ways that encourage the police and law-abiding people to work together with mutual respect and accountability.
6. Community Policing promotes the judicious use of technology, but it also rests on the belief that nothing surpasses what dedicated human beings, talking and working together, can achieve. It invests trust in those who are on the front lines together on the street, relying on their combined judgment, wisdom, and experience to fashion creative new approaches to contemporary community concerns.
7. Community Policing must be a fully integrated approach that involves everyone in the department, with CPOs as specialists in bridging the gap between the police and the people they serve. The Community Policing approach plays a crucial role internally, within the police department, by providing information and assistance about the community and its problems, and by enlisting broad-based community support for the department's overall objectives.
8. Community Policing provides decentralized, personalized police service to the community. It recognizes that the police cannot impose order on the community from outside, but that people must be encouraged to think of the police as a resource they can use in helping to solve contemporary community concerns. It is not a tactic to be applied, then abandoned, but an entirely new way of thinking about the police role in society, a philosophy that also

offers a coherent and cohesive organizational plan that police departments can modify to suit their specific needs.[6]

The logic of community policing implies community empowerment, and its goal is *preventive enforcement*—that is, law enforcement and community groups working together toward being just as creative, organized, and persistent in their crime-preventive tactics and strategies as, say, are narcotics traffickers. The police, furthermore, are called upon to use their resources to work with neighbourhood groups, families, schools, and churches toward developing programmes for positive alternatives for at-risk youngsters.

When the wall separating the people from *their* police is removed, thus allowing the people to become actively involved in enforcing *their* laws, the whole job of law enforcement becomes easier and less hostile. As a practical matter, people will actually come forward and help the police. They will no longer regard them with wariness and distrust. There would be trust between cop and citizen, since both would be working toward a common objective: the safety, protection, and well-being of the community.

All of this can take place, I must however emphasize, only within a macro social, political, and economic environment in which people have reason to hope.

## Weed Out and Punish Rogue Cops

For the idea of community policing to have any real chance at succeeding, residents will have to be able to trust the police, to come to see that the police are not their enemies but their partners. In fact, the very foundation of community policing rests on coordinated partnership between resident groups—block clubs, neighbourhood watches, school and religious groups, social-service agencies, ex- and anti-gang organizations, impact work associations, recreational clubs, outreach groups—and the police in joint efforts against crime.

Most counterproductive to those efforts is a context of persistent hostility toward and distrust of the police. Few issues in community-police relations can destroy or inhibit trust than the beliefs, if not always actual evidence, that the police do not respect the citizens they work for and that the police will readily violate people's rights to due process and the right *not* to be subjected to undue, unnecessary, or excessive force. True enough, many Jamaicans (especially in the middle and upper classes and among the hard-working sectors of the working class) have not been as demanding as they ought in their expectation of proper conduct from the police. Out of sheer exasperation at the seemingly endlessly escalating incidence of crime, many have literally thrown up their hands and said, "Let the police handle it—*in the best way they can.*"

But that "best way" has often meant gross human rights violations at the hands of equally exasperated, ill-trained, and, more troubling, rogue, "bad boy" cops. In carrying out investigations and arrests, all too many of the nation's law officers have done so without regard to the rule of law. The international community has documented cases of the Jamaican police pillaging people's homes, and beating, torturing, and unlawfully executing suspects and presumed collaborators.[7] Not only are these offences criminal, but also they make impossible any real prospects for genuine cooperation between poor communities (the ones most affected by crime) and the police. Poor and working-class communities share an equal distaste for crime—including the street crimes committed against them by similarly situated class members—as do the affluent. But the poor, particularly the black poor, will "circle the wagons" when they feel that a common threat is coming from an altogether unrighteous "Babylon" or that some hostile or aggressive police action is unduly directed toward their "own." None of the ideas for community policing will work, I am saying, if people have a mortal fear of the police.

Improper police conduct is not necessarily a deliberate institutional feature, since at the minimum, the Jamaican police, like the police in all democracies, have rules and stated procedures for the proper way to do police work. More often than not, known cases of gross police brutality are the handiwork of rogue elements, or clique of rogue elements, within the police force. These elements will have to be continually weeded out—and subjected to criminal prosecutions—by internal administrative agencies *and* external community watchdog organizations. Any police officer who seeks to personalize and make as life-or-death combat the "war" against crime belongs to another, primitive era. This is not the age of Dodge City. "Dirty Harry"-type "Trinities" are no longer accepted symbols of good, effective law enforcement.

## Change the Way We Punish

A just criminal justice system will undoubtedly convict some people. It will find them guilty of committing one type of crime or another. The important societal question then becomes: What do we do with the guilty? Put in more compelling, moral terms: What do we *want* to do with *our* guilty? Placing the emphasis on "want" and "our" calls for much self-interested reflection and analysis.

The Russian writer Fyodor Dostoevski once observed that the manner in which a society treats its guilty is a reflection of the society itself. If what we as Jamaicans want to do is to dehumanize, debase, and mete out violence (including hangings) to those our justice system convicts, then it might be that we are, indeed, a violent, brutal people—even if we do not all show it. But that, I am sure, is not the case.

Something even more practical needs to be considered, however. That is, what role should prisons play as a remedy for Jamaica's desperate street-crime problem? Locking up lawbreakers takes them out of circulation, but prison can also reduce a convict's chances of finding a niche in society once freed. Bear in mind that more than 60 percent of the people in prison are there on their second, third, or fourth go-round. They are, in other words, "recidivists." If all we do is lock up or warehouse those whom our system of justice convicts, then as surely as night follows day, so, too, following their inevitable release from prison, someone, or someone's child, mother, sister, brother, is bound to "meet," again, those same convicts down another darkened street, or as they come a climbing over the barbed wire fences and iron gates that were installed precisely to protect "us" from "them."

Before turning our attention specifically to inmate rehabilitation, though, a few what-is-to-be-done things ought to be said as regards the growing illegal drug problem in Jamaica.

## Reinforce Drug-Demand Reduction

Figures or even reliable estimates on how serious a drug-addiction problem Jamaica has are difficult to ascertain, but what is certain is that the country does have a problem. Conjectures are that the population of chronic habitual crack-cocaine users numbers in the thousands. What is also true, as discussed earlier, is that much Jamaican crime is linked with the sale and distribution of illegal drugs.

Hence, a useful remedy for much violent street-crime activity would be either to take the profitability out of the illegal drug trade—for example to legalize hard drugs—or to reduce the demand for them. I come down on the side of demand reduction, essentially so because I am not convinced of the merits of the legalization argument. More troubling for me is that it is being pushed, particularly within official U.S. policy-making circles, by folks whose motives I suspect—mostly right-wing ideologues who, with due respect to noteworthy exceptions like Baltimore's Mayor Kurt Schmoke, an ardent legalization advocate, would just as soon have black people kill off themselves, and each other, with guns and drugs.

Obviously, there is precious little that Jamaica can do to reduce the international demand which drives local illegal drug-trade operations, but greater support could and should be given to community-based programmes geared toward rehabilitating those in the Jamaican society whose criminality is linked to addiction to drugs or alcohol. Such programmes hold the promise of playing an important role in a comprehensive punishment system, as is only now being found out in the United

States and Europe. The programmes offer a paradigm for the blending of effective controls with effective treatment for two main reasons: (1) the prison is an inappropriate place for such programmes, and (2) there is general understanding in most communities that many crime problems are related to mental and emotional problems brought on by, or exacerbated by, drug use.

In Jamaica, one prominent demand-reduction programme is the National Council of Drug Abuse (NCDA). Under the leadership of Chairman Dr. Winston Davidson, the NCDA has developed a variety of integrated demand-reduction strategies. Among them are education, public health strategies, community participation, economic and social development projects, legal assistance, security measures, research and development, and international cooperation.

The Council's approach is to target one representative "problem" community per parish. "Having targeted these communities," Davidson said in an interview with *The Sunday Gleaner* of November 1, 1992, ". . . what we have found is that there is a multiplier effect as a result of the effect of the community development action committee in each of these parishes. And this multiplier effect has affected the surrounding districts and areas . . . ." The NCDA's integrated demand-reduction programme, says Davidson, "was the first of its kind anywhere in the world. The United Nations International Drug country programme has confidence in us and this confidence was manifested by giving us the kind of flexibility to carry out a complex programme [in] this country [i.e., Jamaica]." One effective way to reduce drug and drug-related crimes in Jamaica, then, is for the society to promote and support agencies such as the NCDA.

Having said the above about offenders whose crimes are related to their addictive use of drugs, let me now return to what ought to be done with more "conventional" offenders whom we generally think we have little choice but to send to prison.

## Place Greater Emphasis on Rehabilitation and Education in Prisons

The idea of making prisons places for rehabilitation has never really been seriously tried in Jamaica, or perhaps anywhere. Come election time, Jamaica's two main rival political parties try, among other things, to outdo the other by appearing tough on crime and on the "criminals." Politicians pretty much know they cannot hope to win an election by proclaiming, "I am going to make prisons places where lives can be reclaimed, re-channelled, and redirected." That would be the equivalent of saying, "Vote for me, and I'll raise your taxes." Misgivings aside, rehabilitation does have indisputable merits. One British jurist went so far as to say that, "The best protection society has against crime is the reformation of the offender."[8]

A November 1, 1992, *Sunday Gleaner* piece entitled, "Prisoners Keep Coming Back: Rehabilitation Plan Not Working," tells a story of official Jamaican neglect and abandonment of the idea of rehabilitation. Several persons familiar with the country's prison conditions were interviewed for the piece—including inmates and former inmates. They all believed that "not nearly enough is being done." "There isn't a rehabilitation programme," the story quotes Flo O'Conner, coordinator of the Jamaica Council for Human Rights, as saying. Officials at the Department of Corrections and senior officers at the institutions visited by the *Gleaner* staff admitted that "more needs to be done to rehabilitate inmates." Some of these officials insisted, however, that "lack of funding obstructs the implementation of programmes."

The nation as a whole will have to make a more earnest attempt at reforming and bringing about change in socially and legally condemned lives—youthful lives that somehow got messed up. Perhaps a few of those surface-to-air-missile and DEA dollars, which were not so long ago donated to assist the Jamaican government in its localized version of the "war on drugs," could be diverted into developing new educational and skills-building programmes in the nation's prisons and for strengthening existing ones. Come to think of it, a diversion of this type would also be, in its own way, a "war on drugs." Only this time, instead of law enforcement "winning" by force, the society wins by having re-channelled into another, more productive direction an otherwise wasted life. And just what kind of rehabilitative activities within the prison walls should we consider?

At the very minimum, all prisons should offer, within the confines of the institution, basic-education classes and programmes. Some programmes are, indeed, presently offered, but on a negligible basis. They are understaffed and unable to meet inmate requirements. Exactly how much government actually spends on basic-education programmes— or what proportion of total correctional expenditures goes toward them—is anybody's guess. Nowhere in the 1990 *Statistical Yearbook of Jamaica*, certainly not under "Expenditures for the Correctional System," is there any indication of the dollar amount spent on educational services for inmates. Millions of dollars were spent in the preceding years on new prison construction and on "capital improvements," but nothing showed how much, if anything, went into one of the most basic things the society will simply have to do if it does not want to keep housing and rehousing prisoners: that is, equip them with some kind of literate and functional skills so they may be able to obtain for themselves a life outside of crime.

## Strengthen Prison Industries

At present, three of the island's eight prisons (now referred to in more humane terms as "correctional centres") operate a limited number of prison industries and farm projects. At Tamarind Farm, a minimum-security prison in St. Catherine, cattle and fish farms are run by inmates; at Fort Augusta, also in St. Catherine—the only prison for females—inmates are involved in shoemaking and needlework. Finally, at the South Camp facility, in Kingston, inmates do garment making inside the institution's tailor shop.

The idea of prison industry, or instituting within prisons a system of inmate-worker production which does not duplicate the exploitation of the prison-factory system of late eighteenth and early nineteenth century Europe, is one that can produce positive results. I urge a more focussed and serious concentration on a system of selective industrial undertaking within the Jamaican prison system. Instead of operating essentially traditionally unprofitable concerns, as is now generally the case, a mix of for-profit enterprises producing a wide range of goods and services ought to be considered. Inmates would be paid at rates below the going minimum wage (as I believe is now the case). Wages would be either kept in an escrow account and given upon release, used toward defraying inmates' costs of housing (their room and board), or sent directly to the inmates' families, to victims, or to families of victims. I suggest the below-minimum wage because any work programme in which convicted "murderers and thieves" are seen as getting a better break than "good" law-abiding citizens would be doomed from the outset; it simply would not be politically viable.

Most important, though, the newer type of prison industries I am proposing would be so structured, and the choice of work products so rationalized, so as not to have them compete directly with outside union jobs. This is especially important in view of the prisons' built-in lower costs of production. Nevertheless, organized labour, like private industry, should try to find ways to cooperate with the state in joint prison-industry ventures.

The new or additional prison-industry ventures I recommend would include, as a possible model, the state of Illinois' Correctional Industries, a separate agency within the Department of Corrections which involves inmates in tire recycling, among other things. Scrap tires are collected from state garages and shipped to a correctional facility for processing. This project has been foremost in solid-waste recycling, as mandated by law. The training and experience inmates receive have enhanced their chances of employment after release from prison.

Other industries within the Illinois state system include a meat-processing plant and bakery which supply staff and the inmate population of the entire prison system; a furniture factory supplies desks, chairs, and cabinets to state offices; and a garment factory supplies state workers—police and correctional officers, for example—with uniforms. In addition, there is a microfilming plant, an optical lab, an ethanol plant, and milk-processing operations.

A number of other states have their own prison-industry projects. An Industrial Reformatory in Hutchinson, Kansas, trains 200 inmates each year in fields from auto mechanics to welding. In Texas, more than 4,000 convicts produced a record 42.5 million dollars in goods and services in a single year. Women prisoners in Arizona earn five dollars an hour taking reservations by phone for the Best Western motel chain and in Minnesota, eighty inmates assemble parts for Control Data Corporation, a manufacturer of high-technology components.

All of these prison-industry projects, wherever tried, have managed to remain self-sustaining—and profitable. More important, they have contributed to developing a highly motivated and skilled inmate work force. "[They] give you [an] opportunity to learn what responsibility is about," commented one Minnesota convict. Moreover, as results from one federal government-sponsored study show, inmates who receive training and work experience during their incarceration are less likely to receive misconduct reports in prison. They are more likely to be employed during their halfway house stay (i.e., the time spent between prison and full release back into the community) and are less likely to recidivate than similar inmates who were not trained during their imprisonment.[9]

Jamaican private industry should seek out ways to collaborate with prison-industry ventures, but in ways, I insist, that do not take away job possibilities from law-abiding citizens. In any industry where there is a high labour-intensive component, a little imagination can be brought to bear in finding ways for successful hookups between private industry and the able-bodied and, in most cases, eager work force behind bars.

## Deal Creatively and Constructively With Prison Overcrowding

Past overemphasis (or the wrong emphasis) on punishment has produced in Jamaica, as in the United States, an undesirable boomerang effect: the severe costs associated with prison overcrowding. The unfortunate, costly, and wrong-headed solution to this special problem has been, more often than not, to build yet more prisons.

Estimates vary, but, clearly, Jamaica's prisons presently hold considerably more inmates than they were originally built to house. At the end of 1988, according to an Americas Watch Report, there was a total of 3,697 inmates in all of the island's correctional centres, which was 916 over officially rated capacity.[10] In March 1989, an eight-member task force appointed by the Jamaican Cabinet and chaired by Mr. Gordon Wells, issued a report on prison conditions that contained numerous findings on the sorrowful state of the nation's prisons. The report also made a number of recommendations. Among the most urgent problems cited was overcrowding. Referring to the two main penitentiaries, the St. Catherine District Prison and the General Penitentiary, the report stated that,

> Both institutions are housing twice the number of persons for which they are designed so the cells are grossly overcrowded and in an appalling state. One cell in the District Prison which seemed to be about the size of a large bedroom was housing 53 prisoners. And it must be remembered that when the prisoners are locked in at about 3:30 p.m. each day they are not allowed out again until the next morning.[11]

So coupled with the need to rehabilitate the guilty is the practical need to do something about prison overcrowding. First in this regard is the need for realistic evaluation of the nation's sentencing laws. Is the society in its national legislative process unwisely committing—or, worse, "tying" judges hands—to unnecessary mandatory sentences for offenders whose punishment could be well met in ways other than actual incarceration? From this distance (i.e., from Chicago), it would be impossible to address that specific issue in any great depth for Jamaica, but if the American experience is any guide—where the answer is a resounding "yes"—Jamaica may also be overcommitting offenders to prison. In the hue and cry, sometimes understandable, for politicians, *qua* legislators, to "do something" about crime and to "get the criminals off the street," politicized publics often do manage to get their leaders to enact stiff penalties for crimes. The most favoured is to lock'em up and throw away the key.

There are, undoubtedly, some offenders who must by all means be kept off the streets. And laws that require their mandatory incarceration perform a necessary protective function for the rest of society. But, by the same token, mandatory prison sentences for others, merely because we are angered at their crimes, perform no useful function for the society. We must, therefore, free judges and other appropriate agencies within the judiciary to impose a broad range of intermediate sentences (i.e., sentences short of actual prison terms) for nonviolent offenders.

The type of rational sentencing policy I am recommending is one that would allow sentences to be more tailor-made to fit the offence, the extenuating and aggravating circumstances of the case, and the offender's background and criminal history. To achieve justice, judges would be expected to weigh more than they do now the interests of all parties in the case—the victim, the offender, and the public. For example, punishment and incapacitation would take precedence over rehabilitation in the sentencing of a repeat violent offender who commits crime after violent crime against a person. In contrast, rehabilitation and reintegration would be paramount in the case of a minor property offender who has no prior criminal history but does have a drug habit. At one level, a flexible and yet rational sentencing policy could result in saving a life from further degradation. But, more immediately, it would relieve pressure on available prison space, leaving that space for more dangerous offenders.

What, then, are examples of the type of intermediate punishments to which less-dangerous offenders could be sentenced? Intermediate punishments can be part of a comprehensive system of victim restitution, fines, and community-based punishments or corrections. They are called intermediate because at any time during their imposition, if their terms are violated an offender can be sent forthwith to prison.

Borrowed in part from University of Chicago criminologist Norval Morris,[12] himself an ardent advocate of community-based punishments, the following are some suggested trial options for Jamaica:

- home confinement or house arrest;
- halfway houses that control the convicted offender's nights and weekends while he goes to work or to school each day;
- prisons that allow liberty for work and only for work;
- a wide variety of community-based centres for control and treatment, particularly for drug and alcohol cases;
- a system of means-based fines;
- electronic monitoring;
- shock incarceration or "boot camps," where offenders undergo rigorous physical and mental performance programmes, not so much to "masculinize" or "toughen" them, but to give them a sense of purpose, discipline, belonging, and character; and
- many types of intensive probation.

Many of these intermediate and community-based punishments are being successfully implemented in the United States and Western Europe. The Dutch, for example, are successfully experimenting with a combination of restitution, suspended sentences, and victim compensation. In accordance with guidelines and state law, settlement of criminal damages, sometimes in lieu of a prison sentence, is actively stipulated at all stages in the judicial procedure—arrest, trial, and conviction. In the United States, individual states report gratifying results (specifically, sharply reduced rates of recidivism) from electronic monitoring, boot camps, intensive-probation programmes, and earned-time credits. A passing glance at each of these four programmes might be instructive.

### *Electronic Monitoring (EM)*

Electronic monitoring (also known as electronically monitored home confinement and electronically monitored house arrest) allows law enforcement or corrections personnel to use technology to ensure that offenders are where they are supposed to be when they are suppose to be there. EM is frequently used to augment in-person surveillance patrols; however, EM is also used as a stand-alone surveillance tool.

Here's how the system works. The released offender at all times must be within access of a telephone (on the job or at his home), which monitors his movement through random electronic telephone calls to him. When he is called, the offender must answer personally and report (typically by way of an electronic device assigned or attached to him) on his present activities.

Importantly, EM is not generally viewed as a sanction in and of itself; rather, it's a technology used to supplement offender supervision and case management. An indirect benefit of EM programmes is the offender's ability to work, which allows him to pay child support, restitution, and at least for some of the costs associated with his own supervision. Some programmes have been shown to save a great deal of money over time. For example, the Florida Community Control programme is estimated to have saved more than 160 million dollars over the cost of prison for 60,000 offenders. In addition, the state reports that re-arrest rates for EM participants was 4.6 percent lower than for a matched group of prison releases.[13]

### *Shock Incarceration*

Shock incarceration (SI or "Boot Camp"), which uses the military boot camp experience for redirecting troubled lives, originated in the state of Georgia in 1983. Since then, SI has become a highly popular sentencing option. Twenty-two American states currently have some form of SI programme.

Sometimes referred to as a programme designed to give confused youngsters a "kick in the rear," SI consists of a short period of confinement, usually three to six months, during which offenders are exposed to strict discipline, military-style training (complete with drills and ceremonies), and physical labour. Some programmes, but not all, include education and drug-treatment components. The results of SI are mixed. As far as recidivism rates go, one evaluation study that compared recidivism rates for probationers, parolees, and SI participants reports that, nationally, after twelve months, 51 percent of SI participants were still under supervision, compared to 45 percent for parolees and 67 percent for probationers. Fewer SI participants than probationers or parolees had successfully completed supervision after twelve months. More SI participants (37 percent) were re-arrested at least once during the twelve-month period than offenders from the other two groups. However, the majority of these arrests were for drug trafficking or technical offences. Importantly, SI participants had the fewest arrests for violent or property crimes.[14]

### *Intensive Probation*

In every state, and in the U.S. federal prison system, there are programmes called "Intensive Probation." Their diversity is such that the term has almost ceased to have useful meaning, but their common feature is that more control is exerted over the offender than that described as "normal" probation in that particular jurisdiction. Often these extra control mechanisms involve restrictions on liberty of movement, coercion into treatment programmes, employment obligations, or all three.

One impetus behind such programmes was to create the possibility for judges to avoid further crowding the prisons and jails by giving convicted persons "alternative" punishments. Such punishments were thought to be more acceptable to public opinion since they were sufficiently intrusive and demeaning to be perceived as punitive. But they also held promise of a closer supervision of the offender. Another impetus was the recognition by those running probation services that among those placed on probation were offenders at higher risk of serious criminality than the rest, so that it was sensible to disproportionately allocate supervision and support resources to them.

In 1989, the National Institute of Justice sponsored an evaluation of New Jersey's intensive probation programme. The study found that in terms of crimes committed by those on intensive probation, the results were favourable. Only one in ten was arrested for a new crime (one in twenty for a felony), and only about a third of those whose applications for intensive probation were granted were returned to prison for violations of the probation order.[15]

### *Earned-Time Credit*

One rather practical way to reduce existing prison populations and also accomplish quite effectively the goal of rehabilitation is through expanded use of earned-time credit. A principal reason why the prisons are as crowded as they are today, and why crowding gets worse with time, is recidivism. Research in the United States suggests that recidivism can be reduced (and employment levels increased) among offenders who participate in meaningful educational and work programmes, examples of which I have already mentioned. To reduce the number of inmates returning to prison and, thereby, ease the level of prison overcrowding, the Jamaican government needs to establish a means to get more inmates into meaningful prison programmes that improve their chances of success in the community. A carefully crafted Earned-Time

Credit Programme should succeed in motivating inmates to participate. But motivating inmates may be only half the battle. The other is availability of the work and educational opportunity spaces in which to place them.

If Jamaica should seek to develop these and other types of intermediate punishment (or expand on those it already has) for select groups of offenders, the nation would have much to gain by way of lower prison costs and a greater probability of integrating onetime wasted lives into society.

## Reshape Popular Attitudes Toward the Guilty

The next to last of my recommendations has more to do with changing attitudes than with changing structures. Because of the fundamental class-divided nature of the Jamaican society, Jamaicans have long seen themselves in terms of "us" and "them," despite the country's "out of many, one" credo. "Us" means the respectable, law-abiding, socially white people; and "them" being the black, hooligan class. Some Jamaicans go so far as to invoke a cruel type of class denigration, in which other Jamaicans are presumed "criminals" based on how they look.

At the risk of sounding excessively trite, Jamaicans will not do much about their crime problem until they all come to accept the spiritual brotherhood or sisterhood of all humankind. We are, as Martin Luther King, Jr., used to say in any number of his speeches, "caught in a single garment of destiny." Each person's death, and everyone else's misery, ought to "diminish" all. And that, really, is what nation-building and pride of nation (not, I emphasize, nationalism) is all about—each Jamaican being like every other Jamaican who deserves decent, equal treatment. To deal effectively with the problem of crime, particularly crimes committed by alienated, adrift youngsters, we will all someday have to get to the point where we see that there is no such thing as a bad boy; only that some boys—our boys, our children—ended up thinking badly of themselves and so did indeed "turn" bad.

The country's troubled youths are not animals who were born wicked, evil, or malicious. It is indeed the educated and the well-off, and the kind of society they have built, who made them bad. Having paid for their crimes through incarceration or some other form of punishment, the guilty ask only for a real second chance at life.

## Abolish the Death Penalty

I have saved the most controversial of my recommendations for the last: that is, urging that we do away, once and for all, with the nation's heinous death penalty.

Anyone, I can hear the critics say, who would suggest abolishing the death penalty in a time of rising violent crime must be nuts. As I write, Prime Minister P.J. Patterson is himself going around the country saying in speeches that with violent crime in Jamaica being as serious as it is, there is no way that his government will seek to abolish the death penalty. "Cabinet had spent a great deal of time deliberating the issue and had come to the decision that with the present levels of violent crime, it was not appropriate to abolish capital punishment at this time," says the prime minister.[16] That, precisely, is my point: The seductive grip that capital punishment has on the Jamaican psyche is an additional reason why Jamaica's homicide rates (i.e., exclusive of all other crimes) are among the highest in the world.

The highly respected human rights organization, Amnesty International, points out in its 1989 World Watch on state-sponsored executions that, "executions brutalize those involved in the process . . . ." The death penalty is "the premeditated and cold-blooded killing of a human being by the state. The state can exercise no greater power over a person than that of deliberately depriving him or her of life. At the heart of the case for abolition, therefore, is the question of whether it [the state] has the right to do so."[17]

The death penalty, in other words, is a crime. It's a crime against humanity that is committed and sanctioned by the state. We can never hope to instill respect for life among the "ordinary" people of the land when the nation-state itself insists on as grotesque a display of brutality as a hanging. (Would we dare make hangings from the Spanish Town gallows public or show them on live TV?) If we are to expect all others in the society to respect human life and not deprive another of it, then the state must set the example.

Besides, Jamaica's record on the use of the death penalty typically shows capriciousness and violation of commonly accepted due-process provisions. In some cases, says the Amnesty International report on Jamaica, execution warrants have been issued before prisoners have been able to lodge appeals with the final court of appeals, the Judicial Committee of the Privy Council, in England. "This is very frequently due to the defendant's financial inability to employ a lawyer to prepare the case and file an appeal."[18]

More recently, in a March 5, 1993, report, Amnesty International expressed concern about the fairness of an ongoing judicial review process which reclassifies a number of cases as capital murder, making the defendant a candidate for death row.[19] Current law stipulates that these offenders have twenty-one days to apply for a review of their reclassification by three judges of the Court of Appeal, whose decision is final. Amnesty International claims that most of the prisoners whose cases have been reclassified as capital murder did not have adequate opportunity to consult with legal counsel.

After an unofficial four-year moratorium on executions, begun in April 1976, hangings in Jamaica resumed in August 1980. Since then, fifty-nine prisoners have been executed: twenty-nine between 1980 and 1984; nine in 1985; thirteen in 1986; six in 1987; and two in February 1988. In July 1988, the number of prisoners under sentence of death had risen to 191, one of the highest per capita death row populations in the world.

The nation has indeed been conflicted on the use of the death penalty. According to the history of the political and legal battles in the island over its use, during the moratorium on executions, Parliament had considered the possibility of abolishing the death penalty altogether. On January 30, 1979, the House of Representatives voted by a narrow margin to retain capital punishment but recommended that all existing death sentences be reviewed. On February 9, 1979, the Senate voted in favour of suspending the death penalty for a further eighteen months while the issue was considered in more detail.

In June 1979, the then minister of justice established a committee to consider whether the death penalty was an appropriate punishment for murder. The Committee on Capital Punishment and Penal Reform (known as the Fraser Committee, after its chairperson, Aubrey Fraser) submitted its report to the government in December 1981, stating that it was "... of the opinion that death as a penalty for murder should be abolished."[20] It acknowledged, however, that public sentiment was very much in favour of the death penalty. The committee recommended that moves toward abolition should be undertaken "as part of a comprehensive system of penal reform which should commence without delay." As a first step, the committee recommended that, "All sentences of death imposed prior to December 31, 1980, which was the date originally prescribed for submitting the Committee's report . . . should be statutorily commuted to sentences of life imprisonment." The committee further recommended that the application of the death penalty be modified to restrict it to a limited class of homicide, and that for an interim period of five years, capital punishment should be retained only for murder committed by use of a firearm or explosive.

The Fraser Committee's research team reviewed the cases of forty of the eighty-one prisoners then on death row. It found that almost all of them came from the lower socioeconomic sectors of the society, that the majority of them had little or no education, that most were first-time offenders, and that many appeared not to have had the benefit of adequate counsel. Amnesty International's own research, based on contact with lawyers representing prisoners under sentence of death and an examination of information on many prisoners' cases, supported these findings. Most prisoners were too poor to pay for private legal representation, Amnesty International found. Rather, they were represented by court-appointed, newly qualified, and inexperienced legal-aid lawyers at trial and local appeal. The fees received by legal-aid lawyers were extremely low, and there was no legal aid for appeals to the Privy Council. For pursuing such appeals, prisoners were, therefore, entirely dependent on lawyers providing their services for free.

In 1982, by a majority of three to two, the Privy Council dismissed appeals in the cases of Noel Riley and four others who had been sentenced to death in 1975 and 1976, the period during which executions had been suspended. The prisoners had argued that the issuing of warrants for their execution after the delay caused by the suspension of hangings amounted to "inhuman or degrading punishment or treatment" and was in violation of the Jamaican Constitution. The majority rejected the appeal on a point of law, but two judges entered vigorous dissenting opinions in which they found that the appellants had been subjected to a "cruel and dehumanizing experience" and that their execution after such a delay would amount to "inhuman treatment." The five prisoners were executed three months after the decision was handed down.

Few death penalty cases submitted to the Privy Council are ever given a full hearing, since they are normally rejected at the stage of "seeking leave to appeal." However, in October 1987 the Privy Council agreed to hear appeals in three separate cases of Jamaican prisoners who had been convicted and sentenced to death on the basis of poor identification evidence. This involved the accused having been identified by only one witness in poor light, and at considerable distance from the witness, and with no other evidence against the accused being presented. The appeals were based on claims that the trial judges had failed to direct the juries adequately on the weight they should attach to such evidence. In similar cases in the past, the Privy Council had refused to "leave to appeal." But the rising number of cases raising the issue of judges instructions prompted the Council to consider the matter a point of law and of general public importance, thereby bringing it within their jurisdiction. One of the prisoners whose appeal was to be heard, Junior Reid, had been scheduled for execution in June 1986; he was granted a last-minute stay. Trevor Ellis, a prisoner convicted on the basis of similar evidence, had his petition for leave to appeal to the Privy Council rejected in 1985 and came within hours of being executed in March 1988, before being granted a last-minute stay of execution.

In some cases, there have been long delays between the hearing of an appeal by the Jamaican Court of Appeal and the delivery of the written reasons for judgment. This has prevented the prisoners from lodging any further appeals. A written decision from the Court of Appeal is the basis for a further appeal to the Privy Council. Earl Pratt and Ivan Morgan, both convicted and sentenced to death in January 1979 (the period during which executions were suspended while parliament and the Fraser Committee considered the question of abolition), communicated their case to the Human Rights Committee set up under the International Covenant on Civil and Political Rights. The men alleged among other things, that the long delays in the proceedings against them, particularly a delay of nearly four years in the issuing of the written judgment of the Jamaican Court of Appeals, violated their rights of due process under Article 14 of the Covenant. In dismissing their appeals in 1986, the Privy Council expressed "disquiet" over the two having been under sentence of death for so long. Both came within hours of being executed on two occasions, in February 1987 and February 1988.

There have been cases in which applications for leave to appeal to the Jamaican Court of Appeal have been treated as the full hearing of the appeal and dismissed orally, with no indication from the judges that they would put their reasons into writing. Such a practice prevents the prisoner from being able to pursue further appeals to the Privy Council.

A number of prisoners on death row in 1989, according to Amnesty International, were reported to have developed signs of mental illness while on death row. And at least one mentally ill person had been executed. Stafford Pyne was executed on June 28, 1983, five days after a psychiatrist had diagnosed a schizophrenic illness. Pyne had a history of mental illness both in prison and before his arrest and had been treated at Bellevue Hospital at the age of fourteen.

Philip Grey, sentenced to death in March 1981 and declared insane by a consultant psychiatrist in February 1986, was scheduled for execution in November 1987. His sentence was commuted after the Jamaica Council for Human Rights sent a petition to the Governor General enclosing a copy of the psychiatrist's report. Other prisoners with a history of mental illness before their arrest remain on death row, according to Amnesty International.

A society which metes out the ultimate act of barbarity on its helpless and most vulnerable members is one which cannot possibly hope to repair itself of the damage inflicted on it through violent street crime. Furthermore, when a state convicts prisoners without affording them appropriate legal safeguards, it denies the right to due process and equality before the law. The irrevocable punishment of death removes not only the dead person's right to seek legal redress from wrongful conviction, but also the judicial system's capacity to correct its errors.

Like killings that take place outside the law, the death penalty denies the value of human life. By violating the right to life, it removes the foundation for the realization of all rights enshrined in the Universal Declaration of Human Rights. As the Human Rights Committee set up under the International Covenant on Civil and Political Rights has recognized, "The right to life . . . is the supreme right from which no derogation is permitted even in time of public emergency which threatens the life of the nation . . . ." In a general comment on Article Six of the Covenant issued in 1982, the Committee concluded that "all measures of abolition [of the death penalty] should be considered as progress in the enjoyment of the right to life . . . ."[21]

Over the years, scores of Jamaicans have been executed on Jamaica's Spanish Town gallows for the stated purpose of preventing crime, especially the crime of murder. Some 800 plus murders in that tiny island in 1980 is proof positive that, in Jamaica, the death penalty has not accomplished the objective of deterrence. Study after study in diverse countries have failed to find convincing evidence that the death penalty has any unique capacity to deter others from committing particular crimes. A 1988 survey of research findings on the relation between the death penalty and homicide rates, conducted for the United Nations, concludes: "This research has failed to provide scientific proof that executions have a greater deterrent effect than life imprisonment. Such proof is unlikely to be forthcoming. The evidence as a whole still gives no positive support to the deterrent hypothesis."[22]

Undeniably, the death penalty, by permanently "incapacitating" a prisoner, prevents that person from repeating the crime. But there is no way to be sure that the prisoner would indeed have repeated the crime if allowed to live, nor is there any need to violate the prisoner's right to life for the purpose of incapacitation. Dangerous offenders can be kept safely away from the public without resorting to execution, as shown by the experience of many abolitionist nations. And to those who would ask, "Why should taxpayers' money be spent to keep alive in prison a convicted murderer?" I have a surprising answer. My guess is that, based on the experience in the United States,[23] that the right-to-appeal/review process in Jamaica, guaranteed, at least in theory, under current death penalty law, typically generates public costs that are much more expensive than would be the case for imposition of life sentences with a differently crafted right-to-appeal process.

Every society seeks protection from crime, but far from being a solution, the death penalty gives the erroneous impression that "firm measures" are being taken against crime. The death penalty diverts attention from the more complex measures that are really needed. In the words of former British Prime Minister Edward Heath, no left-wing ideologue, ". . . the constant emphasis on capital punishment is preventing us from giving real attention and resources to the problems of crime in a modern democracy. . . . We must recognize that if we really are to tackle the penal problems of the country we must turn our attention to that, instead of automatically saying that the answer is hanging and flogging."[24]

As real antidotes for the crime of murder, what is to be done is for the Jamaican society at large to seriously contemplate genuine violence-prevention measures such as, for example:

- early intervention into families afflicted by the pain of drugs, crime, poverty, domestic violence, and general dysfunctionality;
- training in schools and community workshop-like settings for nonviolent responses to interpersonal conflicts;

- restoration of broken families;
- increased aid to provide special education for children with learning disabilities;
- identification and early help for children and adolescents with problems of mental retardation and brain damage, which they may have gotten from birth defect, trauma, malnutrition, or abuse;
- making everyone in the society whole.

Again, these will all incur some costs, but significantly less than the costs of continued high levels of violent crimes.

Coretta Scott King, whose husband and mother-in-law were both murdered, best sums up the sentiment of all reasonable and well-thinking people on the issue of the death penalty—including, by the way, several American-based abolitionist groups whose ranks consist of family members of murder victims. "An evil deed," Mrs. King said, "is not redeemed by an evil deed of retaliation."[25]

There is hope for altering Jamaica's crime situation. But that hope does not lie in the use of punishment that is cruel and inhumane nor in the firepower of the country's security forces. Better police armaments and more executions will not solve deep-rooted problems of dispossession and despair. Jamaica's hope lies in building a more just and humane society.

In the next and final chapter we look at some of the broader cultural forces that have nurtured and reinforced the myth of the "badman" in Jamaica. I do have a reason why I decided to close with an examination of that troubling misnomer.

# 6
# Beyond the Badman Mystique

*. . . Gunslingah to raas.*
*Is a starbwai dis!*
—From Michael Thelwell,
*The Harder They Come*

*We were not able to choose the mess we have to live in—this collapse of a whole Society—but we can choose our way out.*
—C.L.R. James

After all I that I have said in the foregoing chapters about violent street crimes being the result of alienating social and economic forces which impact disproportionately on so many within the Jamaican society, one other factor, finally, must also be considered: that is, the influence of popular culture, and popular values, in shaping images of certain violent offenders. Something there is about us Jamaicans that causes us, perhaps unwittingly, to mythologize rogues, renegades, and badmen.

Maybe it all has to do with our collective past, our strange affection for the desperado being the result of a leftover suspicion of legal authority. That onetime healthy practice of mass defiance was indeed passed on to today's Jamaicans by ancestors whose bruised and broken backs bore witness to the oppressive behaviour of the law. There can be little doubting that the massa's criminal and civil law, along with his various enforcement agencies (police, courts, prisons), did work against the best interests of the black Jamaican masses.

So with rightful justification our people learned to revere Sam Sharpe's insurgency and the Maroon's rebellious heroics. We proudly, and loudly, proclaim as one of our very own a man who was at one time among the United States' "most wanted." In fact, a young Jamaican nation, early into its independence, made Marcus Garvey one of its national heroes. The picture of Marcus Garvey defiantly standing up to the symbols of late-1920s Jamaican colonial authority—the local legislature, big-time Duke Street barristers and Queen's Councils (including the revered Norman Manley), and *The Gleaner*—then being scurried off to do time in the Spanish Town prison, is held up to schoolchildren everywhere, especially to those with even the tiniest drop of African blood in their veins, as the quintessence of black contumacy.

Resistance and defiance are, in other words, significant throwback attitudinal traits that define a collective Jamaican self. Following emancipation and the 1938 rebellions, resistance and defiance were turned into popular embrace of would-be Robin Hoods, which often got translated into perverse hero worship of dark and mysterious characters who, with guns ablazing, would face down the police. In fact, most Jamaicans can recall stories—often told by good, law-abiding parents (usually fathers)—of the exploits of the legendary Rhygin. One of the most popular pieces of cultural work to come out of Jamaica was a movie, and a subsequent novel, glorifying him.

So deeply ingrained is the tendency to endow with mythic qualities anyone who would challenge the forces of legal oppression that it stayed on within the society long after outward changes had taken place in the postcolonial institutional order, that is, after the formal withdrawal of the British in 1962. Perhaps collective suspicion of legal authority could have been rechannelled, or redeployed, into some other useful direction if after independence we had tried harder to incorporate into our justice system and labour laws elements of this peculiar historical experience of resistance. (That is why, coincidentally, the debate on Jamaica's entire postcolonial legal order must continue, including, but certainly not limited to, judicial reform.)

Be that as it may, the unwitting persistence of the badman motif now weighs heavily on Jamaica's insistent crime problem. I am struck by it as over the years I have observed how the Jamaican media, including the respected *Gleaner*, handles celebrated renegade crime stories. Take for example their treatment of the murderous carryings-on of the much-vaunted "Natty" Morgan, in 1991.

One artist's sketch I saw of him in an edition of *The Sunday Gleaner* illustrates my concern. The sketch was clearly not intended as a suspect profile which might have been used to assist the police, through citizen cooperation, at apprehending him. Not at all. What we were looking at (at least what I saw) was the evocative portrayal of a rebel: tightly drawn lips; sharp, steely, uncompromising eyes sunk deep into a sullen, defiant, born-to-raise-hell face. This was all set against the barrel of the omnipresent gun—that symbol of maximum, all-mus'-bow-down power in a twisted, machismo society—from which ascends a halo-ish cloud of fresh smoke. It was a picture filled with dark imagery, misguidedly playing on the Jamaican subconscious tendency to defy.

The problem with that portrayal is that any number of Jamaica's troubled, alienated youth could take one look at it and come away filled with awe—and much seditious imaginings.

One other effect is that the police, seeing themselves pitted against this larger-than-life people's badman, become caught up in a personalized, primeval battle with, as they see it, a living force of evil. Ordinary law enforcement gets elevated to a biblical struggle between the forces of light and darkness, good and evil. It's a duel to the finish, in which the object is for the police to bring in their bounty more dead than alive, *fi mek dem si seh ah wi ah de baddis*—which they eventually did with "Natty" Morgan. It is a scenario of badman enforcers against legendary, mythic badman, one in which law enforcement takes on the lawless in a frontier-type confrontation—this in a society where a tradition of defiance is being constantly reinforced and given vibrancy from underneath.

How does the society extricate itself from the badman dilemma? I submit that the most obvious starting point is to seek ways to disenthral ourselves of all residual elements that, consciously or unconsciously, promote a badman mystique. Not an easy task, to say the least, in a society steeped in the language of violence, especially the sexual violence prattled in the mumbo-jumbo lyrics of some of our current dancehall "songs." Here, more worrisomely, the violence is, more often than not, directed at mothers, wives, sisters, and daughters, and at the police, as new Commissioner of Police Colonel Trevor MacMillan has been forcefully reminding the nation.

In so many ways, the Jamaican society will either have to start over or embark on a journey of rediscovery. In any case, one begins with the educative process. All of us who teach—not just paid classroom instructors, but more important preachers, political leaders, journalists, media people, artists, entertainers—need now to begin a generations-long task of presenting appropriate images to our people and to instill within them a new community ethos. That ethos I referred to earlier as the communitarian agenda, meaning, an agenda which places emphasis on community efforts to achieve the overall well-being of the whole, and which emphasizes mutual respect and obligations.

Many recent developments in the Jamaican society suggest, among other things, an increasing loss of faith in the island's two main rival political parties. In some circles, particularly within sectors of the influential middle class, a growing sense of apathy toward *all* organized political structures seems to have taken hold, as the late Professor Stone's polls were beginning to show. The relatively low voter turnout in the 1993 general election (under 70 percent, compared to well over 80 percent in previous election years) only proves the point. People at all levels of the society no longer fervently believe that government alone can solve the nation's political, economic, and moral crisis. So the time may indeed be right for a movement that combines moral suasion and political action to bring about a greater sense of responsibility in all Jamaicans. We cannot expect to win—whether it's in global economic competition or in the "fight" against crime—with a primitive everyone-take-for-yourself-and-run attitude, or take a say-as-you-like, do-as-you-like approach to social existence.

Only a broad plan of action for bolstering the foundations of the society—the family, the schools (public and private), the media, and the institutions of community life—can rescue us from the depredations of the badman. A communitarian agenda for the common good calls for strengthening of moral education in the nation's schools, encouraging moral leadership through things such as national service, a restoration of civility, and a willingness at all levels of the society to distinguish right from wrong.

But, critics might query: Whose morals will be taught? Well, Jamaicans, most Jamaicans anyway, happen to share a set of basic, commodified values which are quite apart and distinct from the values of commodified culture. We share most notably, for instance, the value of tolerance. And for this one has only to look at the plethora of denominations and religious faiths that exist alongside each other in one tiny island. Contrast that with the situation in the Balkans, where the Bosnians, who comprise no more than three major ethno-religious groupings, are slaughtering each other in a brutal war to decide which group lives where. Jamaicans also share a general sense of neighbourliness and sharing, and a fundamental respect for democratic decision making. All of these can be incorporated (or reincorporated) into instruction and into the culture of schools.

Under a new communitarian agenda, we would have to correct false cultural readings of history. Rhygin was no Robin Hood. And the liberation struggles of Sam Sharpe, Cudjoe, Nanny, the Maroons, and Marcus Garvey had no equivalence, none whatsoever, with the destructive, self-serving, predatory criminal violence of the modern-day badman, whose only "cause" is himself. We will further have to tell the children the sad, ironic truth that, not only are the "Sandokans" and "Natty" Morgans the ordinary, garden-variety thugs a broken society has produced, but that, when we get right down to it, they reflect the individualistic, capitalist greed of the larger society.

A new moral tone for the society, one which emphasizes both rights *and* responsibilities, is the ultimate bulwark against crime. That tone will have to come from literally hundreds of community efforts, not from parliamentary or political-Party action. The gap between the haves and the have-nots, between "rights and rightness," cannot be closed, says communitarian thinker and sociologist Amitai Etzioni, "without a moral vocabulary—one that invokes principles of decency, duty, responsibility, and the common good."[1]

A civilized society assumes peace, order, and mutual respect as the norm, and considers violence, any violence (including the violence of the death penalty), unacceptable. But more to the point, a civilized society educates its children to be peaceful, orderly, disciplined, and respectful to others and of the conventions that lubricate our social transactions and to live and work together with minimum friction. We certainly cannot expect the Jamaican society to turn "on a dime" in bringing about, overnight, this new moral order. But the journey can at least begin—or start anew.

# Epilogue

In this brief work, I have tried to show that one of the results of Jamaica's disarticulated or one-sided developmentalism has been a condition of severe inequalities between the society's haves and have-nots. Consolidated structural inequalities—with close to 80 percent of the Jamaican people being locked out from the gains that the other 20 percent (or less) enjoy—have produced not only obvious deprivation, but despair, anger, and alienation.

A limited number of expedient options for escape from a life of joblessness, poverty, and wretchedness have been more or less available to those so affected. One is to migrate, first from the hillsides of the "country" into "town" (usually to Kingston, the nation's capital city), then, when that proves economically futile, on to the metropolitan countries of the North. Another is to forge clientelistic links with one of the country's two main rival political parties, the outcome of which has been ferocious intraclass battles which have left basically unchallenged a political-economic system that continues to reproduce poverty and deprivation. Yet a third option is to engage in activities that are most destructive of cooperative social existence—petty acts of hustling, then on to street crime or drug dealing, with their natural built-in tendency toward waste, death, and destruction. Exercise of either of the three options, I argued, usually follows on the heels of desperation.

Not wanting to dismiss the situation as one without hope, I did suggest some short- and long-term solutions for Jamaica's crime problem. I presented sets of intervention and crime-prevention strategies, not as do-good programmes, but as projects designed in the larger interest and self-preservation of the society. I also argued for a transformation in the way law enforcement and punishment are carried out. Involvement of the grass roots in police decision making and in implementing progressive modes of punishing and rehabilitating the guilty were suggested as additional, imaginative ways for reducing crime.

Jamaica's jailed and imprisoned are, I have reason to believe, folks who desire meaningful participation in the larger social order of which they are a part. The nation's jailed and imprisoned, along with those who are at risk of becoming so, are folks—able-bodied young men for the most part—who would prefer a chance to care in socially approving ways for themselves and their families. They would rather be "burdened" with the responsibilities of productive citizenship—working every day and paying taxes—than being beset by the penalties of crime.

It is not a dissolute culture of violence and dependency which holds back, in a life of crime, so many in Jamaica's shanty towns. But acculturation and concentrated indoctrination of accepted values of perseverance, discipline, delayed gratification, and hard work as the route to eventual success will achieve little by way of lifting the disenfranchised unless they are also presented with some measure of meaningful, structural access.

In the final analysis, only when all of us who make up the Jamaican society—the Jamaica without borders, as our leaders now like to put it—have restored a sense of civility to national life, to really look out for each other in a renewed communitarian spirit, can we hope to have a nation without crime.

# Postscript

Some two years have elapsed since I committed to publication, first in Jamaica then in the United States, *The Jamaican Crime Scene.* As any astute observer of developments in Jamaica and the wider Caribbean knows, a lot can happen—and indeed has happened—in Jamaica in the space of two seemingly short years. Significantly, though, not much has happened to change in a positive direction the rather bleak, though by no means pessimistic, crime situation I tried objectively to analyze here.

In some ways, the situation may have gotten worse. Numbers and rates of violent crime have shown increases in each of the last two years (1993 and 1994) over the immediately preceding years. Whether these crimes are results of mostly so-called family and/or "domestic disputes," as Jamaican law-enforcement authorities vigorously maintain, is by no means clear. The implication of that official contention, by the way, would be that the local crime situation is incapable of being changed through larger, structural policies. Preliminary results from research I conducted with University of the West Indies students in the summer of 1994 suggest, however, that Jamaicans who rob, maim, and kill other Jamaicans, especially in select urban areas, really do not "know" their victims, at least not in the classic *domestic* sense.

Importantly, two principal developments in the last two years have further compounded the Jamaican crime scene. One of them I discussed in this book as an indication of more troubling things to come: that is, the problem of returning Jamaicans with established overseas criminal careers in, more often than not, illegal drug trafficking. The hundreds of deportees shipped back to Jamaican soil in the last two years have added a whole new policing "nightmare." Unable to achieve re-entry into the Metropolitan countries, many deportees have succeeded in making, as at no other time in the country's history, narcotics truly "big-time" business in the island. And with cocaine trafficking, particularly in crack cocaine, has come more violent crime.

A far more profound and paradoxical, though related, development is also shaping the Jamaican *urban* crime scene. It's the further erosion, in isolated constituencies, of garrison politics. The onetime pact between fierce ghetto loyalists and powerful Party leaders has in recent times come under severe strain. That clientelist pact, also discussed at some length, served simultaneously as (1) the source of political power for charismatic politicians such as Party leaders Edward Seaga and Michael

Manley and (2) enforcer of first resort of a type of rough discipline in ghetto neighbourhoods. Violence, for one, could be used among partisan street toughs *only* in the service of partisan ends—mostly to gain or defend political turf.

The pact held (for some twenty-five years) as long as the leaders of the island's two principal, rival political parties—Mr. Seaga's Jamaica Labour Party (JLP) and Mr. Manley's (now Prime Minister P.J. Patterson's) People's National Party (PNP)—were indeed able to deliver, though a rigidly structured patronage chain, political goods. Inability to do so, or availability of illegal goods outside the patronage chain, would mean outbreak of potentially uncontrollable violent trouble. Both outcomes occurred during the last year or so, giving a new twist to the trajectory of crime, violence, and politics in the Jamaican society.

Most notably, JLP leader Edward Seaga was totally ineffective at bringing to heel, throughout much of 1994, street toughs in his own tightly controlled West Kingston political constituency. Several of the area's youths have found much more lucrative, and indeed more violent, ways to survive than in fighting vicious political street battles. The upshot has been waves of violence which, generally, have had more to do with illegal drugs and guns than with defending party turf. Added to that have been Mr. Seaga's own troubles in continuing as "maximum don" of a party that is deeply divided, and the governing PNP's dubious attempts at reforming a spoils system, which did also bring them into power.

# Notes

## *Preface*

1. "We'll Tackle It Together, Government and Opposition Unite To Fight Crime," *Caribbean News* (November 17, 1992).
2. "Proposal to Unify Police and Military Criticized," *ibid.*

## *Prologue*

1. *Bureau of Justice Statistics Bulletin* (Washington, D.C.: U.S. Department of Justice, October 1992).
2. Erik Larson, "The Story of a Gun," *The Atlantic* (January 1993), pp. 48–78.
3. In a federal retrial of the case, two of the four officers were found guilty of violating King's civil rights by the level of excessive force they had used to arrest him. That decision was essentially arrived at after the jury had viewed an eighty-odd-second videotaped recording of the officers beating and stomping King as he lay on the ground.
4. Cited in Erik Larson, *op. cit.*
5. "Bullets Fly and Teens Fall During Violent 28 Hours," *Chicago Tribune* (March 27, 1993).
6. "Children Who Live With Death," *Chicago Tribune* (April 4, 1993)
7. Erik Larson, *op. cit.*
8. "German Tourist Killed in Miami . . . ," *Chicago Tribune* (April 4, 1993).
9. See, e.g., James Q. Wilson and Richard J. Herrnstein, *Crime and Human Nature* (New York: Simon & Schuster, 1985).
10. Cited in Alan Bullock and Oliver Stallybrass (eds.) *The Harper Dictionary of Modern Thought* (New York: Harper and Row, 1977) p. 298.
11. But see, e.g., William K. Tabb (ed.), *The Future of Socialism* (New York: Monthly Review, 1990); Samir Amin, et al., *Transforming the Revolution* (New York: Monthly Review, 1990).
12. Norman P. Girvan, "Rethinking Development: Out Loud," in Judith Wedderburn (ed.), *Rethinking Development* (Mona: Consortium Graduate School of Social Sciences, University of the West Indies, 1991), p. 2.
13. "Czech Prostitution is 'Price of Freedom,' " *Chicago Tribune* (May 2, 1993).
14. *Uniform Crime Reports for the United States 1991* (Washington, D.C.: U.S. Government Printing Office).
15. Of course, in any country, police efforts are typically directed toward solving only those crimes that come directly to their attention as they patrol neighbourhood streets or are reported to them. If all the crimes that are not generally reported to the police (e.g., crimes involving domestic violence, rape, and petty larceny) should ever find their way into the official statistics,

an altogether more frightening crime picture would emerge. In Jamaica, notes one rather astute observer, "less than 20 percent of crimes committed are actually reported and recorded." See Delroy Chuck, "Is the Criminal Justice System Adequately Prepared?" *Sunday Gleaner* (January 10, 1993). These unreported crimes become the "dark figures" of crime.

16. See "Human Rights in Jamaica," An Americas Watch Report (New York, 1986).
17. Quoted in Tony Platt, "Beyond the Canon, With Great Difficulty," paper presented at the annual meeting of the Academy of Criminal Justice Sciences, Kansas City, Missouri, March 1993.

## *Chapter 1*

1. Orlando H. Patterson, *The Children of Sisyphus* (Kingston, Jamaica: Bolivar, 1974).
2. "Shooting at a Jersey Picnic Linked to Jamaican Politics," *New York Times* (August 6, 1985).
3. "A Crackdown on Criminal Gangs from Jamaica," *Los Angeles Times* (October 21, 1987).
4. "U.S. Seizes Air Jamaica Jet in Drug Case," *New York Times* (August 8, 1985).
5. "Church Shootout Suspect Walks out of Hospital," *The [Waukegan, Illinois] News-Sun* (March 9, 1987).
6. Of course, the U.S. illegal drug market was on the rise long before its penetration by Jamaicans in the 1980s. Jamaicans came to constitute only one, albeit significant, set of players in the underground American drug economy. The 1990s would see, in the upper Manhattan, New York, area street drug sales come under the relatively unrivalled control of gangs from the Dominican Republic. Jamaican gangs are still seen, however, as the cleverest, the most violent, and the most organized.
7. "Jamaican Drug Gangs Thriving in Big U.S. Cities," *The New York Times* (July 19, 1987).
8. "The 'Velcro Don': Wiseguys Finish Last," *Newsweek* (April 13, 1992). By the end of the 1980s, American law enforcement had successfully prosecuted or was hot on the "heels" of several within the top ranks of the leading posses, notably so in the Miami and New York areas. A number of them the American authorities had shipped back to Jamaica.
9. George Wayne, "The Bust of the Brutal Jamaican Posses," *The Daily Gleaner* (November 16, 1987).
10. Franklin McKnight, "Posse Backlash Affects Jamaicans in U.S.," *The Daily Gleaner* (December 27, 1987), p. 15.
11. Quoted in Franklin McKnight, "Posse Under Press Searchlight Again," *The Daily Gleaner* (January 31, 1988), p. 1C.
12. Peter Tosh was co-founder, with Bob Marley and Bunny Wailer, of the popular early 1960s reggae group, "The Wailers." The group split in the middle 1970s when Marley decided to go solo. Long regarded as a Rastafarian iconoclast and fierce critic of the Jamaican establishment, Tosh had frequent "run-ins" with the local police. While at his suburban Kingston home with friends and family on Friday night, September 11, 1978, three men

"dropped in." They were not exactly strangers, since one of the men, Dennis "Leppo" Lobbam, was a known "hanger on" among reggae artists. The men pulled guns and demanded money. They told everyone to lie down on the floor and than began firing wildly, killing three people, including Tosh, and injuring four others. The men took a little cash and some jewelry, then left.

13. Dudley Allen, "Violent Crime in Jamaica," in Rosemary and Gary Brana-Shute (eds.), *Crime and Punishment in the Caribbean* (Gainsville: University of Florida Press, 1980).
14. William Wilbanks, "Homicide in Jamaica," paper presented at the Annual Meeting, American Society of Criminology, Washington, D.C., 1978.
15. The more blatant discrepancies include the following: (1) Up through the 1970s, tallying of known or reported crimes was in fiscal years; sometime in the 1980s, it switched to calendar years. (2) Only since the 1980s has the offence of rape been separated from other sex-related crimes whereas robbery was always counted as either "assault" or "larceny." (3) Judicial and legislative redefinition of manslaughter occurred. (4) Crime counts were dependent on which of three or four agency reports consulted.
16. Terry Lacey, *Violence and Politics in Jamaica, 1960–1970* (Totowa, N.J.: Frank Cass & Co. Limited, 1977).
17. Among other useful things, a country's crime rate allows for statistical comparisons over time and across regional and international boundaries. It is computed as follows:

$$\frac{\text{Number of reported crimes}}{\text{Total population}} \times 100{,}000$$

18. *Uniform Crime Reports for the United States 1980* (Washington, D.C.: U.S. Government Printing Office). A more revealing statistic than the rate of reported crime is the rate of victimization, i.e., for number of people saying they were victimized by a crime but chose not to report it to the police. According to the *Bureau of Justice Statistics Bulletin* (*op. cit.*), approximately 40,252,000 such incidents occurred in the States in 1980, for a victimization rate of 20,130 offences per 100,000 population. As far as I am able to tell, no similar systematic victimization survey has ever been conducted in Jamaica. I doubt, however, that those rates would be anywhere close to the United State's rate.
19. "629 Murders Recorded in 1992," *Sunday Gleaner* (January 3, 1993).
20. Mass killers differ from serial killers in style and *modus operandi*. The former slays a number of victims *en masse* whereas the latter does so one at a time, usually over an extended period.
21. See, e.g., literature cited in Jack Levin and James Alan Fox, *Mass Murder* (New York: Plenum, 1985); and Eric W. Hickey, *Serial Murderers and Their Victims* (Pacific Grove: Brooks/Cole, 1991).
22. See, e.g., Martin Daly and Margo Wilson, *Homicide* (New York: Aldine, 1988), chapter 6.
23. Susan Brownmiller, *Against Our Will: Men, Women and Rape* (New York: Bantam, 1975).

24. Marcia Ann Gillespie, "In the Matter of Rape," *Essence* (January 1992), p. 61. A prime, if extreme, example of rape as a crime of male power and domination are the ongoing atrocities in the Balkans, where according to any number of reliable news sources male Serbian forces have engaged in systematic rapes (some 20,000 between 1992 and early 1993) and deliberate impregnations of Muslim women in the name of "ethnic cleansing" in Bosnia. See, e.g., Slavenka Drakulic, *The Balkan Express: Fragments from the Other Side of War* (New York: W.W. Norton, 1993).
25. Other manifestations of broader system pathology (or "breakdown"), though of a different order of magnitude, would include the dramatic increase in acts of system-directed violence—such as, for example, food rebellions and violent worker unrests.
26. The folkloric character was one of Jamaica's earliest badmen. He was acclaimed, especially among the working class, for what were believed to be his Robin Hood-like exploits and bloody showdowns with the police. The 1972 film, "The Harder They Come," gives an uneven novelized version of his life; so does the book by Michael Thelwell, *The Harder They Come* (New York: Grove Press, 1980), which was essentially an adaptation of the film.

## *Chapter 2*

1. Michel Foucault, *Discipline and Punish* (New York: Vintage, 1979), p. 94.
2. Quoted in Leon Radzinowicz and Joan King, *The Growth of Crime* (New York: Basic Books, 1977), p. 65.
3. See, e.g., Ken Pryce, "Towards a Caribbean Criminology," *Caribbean Issues,* 2 (No. 2, 1976), pp. 26–34.
4. See, e.g., Eric Hobsbawm, *Bandits* (New York: Delacorte, 1969); Douglas Hay, et al., *Albion's Fatal Tree: Crime and Society in Eighteenth-Century England* (New York: Pantheon, 1975); Tony Platt, "Street Crime: A View from the Left," *Crime and Social Justice,* 9 (1978), pp. 26–34.
5. Had it not been for a sprinkling of East Indians, the percentage of incarcerated Afro-Jamaicans would easily have been 100 percent. East Indians were brought into Jamaica as indentured servants following Abolition. Unlike other Caribbean nations (notably Trinidad & Tobago and Guyana), "pure" or unmixed East Indians constitute only a small percentage of the total Jamaican population (less than 4 percent). They have for the most part, however, shared a fate of dispossession with the masses of their Afro-Jamaican brethren.
6. In 1989, the most recent year for which there are available government data, total recurrent and capital expenditure for national security, law enforcement, and corrections was 290 million dollars, or roughly 14 percent of the country's Gross Domestic Product.
7. Upton Sinclair, *The Jungle* (New York: Penguin, 1980), p. 165.
8. See Bernard Headley, "Structural Correlates of Dependent Capitalist Development and Increase in Criminality in Jamaica," Ph.D. dissertation (Washington, D.C.: Howard University, 1982).
9. Although maximizing corporate profits, the pattern of multinational bauxite-alumina investments in Jamaica served to undercut the establishment of

internal industrial linkages and the spread of employment. Elements of this pattern—vertical integration across the ocean (bauxite mining in Jamaica and aluminium smelting in Arkansas); multinational sourcing of output (milling sugar cane from Jamaica, Guyana, and Barbados); the preponderance of inputs imported from parent companies and overseas suppliers; capital-intensive techniques of production—served to reduce company costs and pushed up profits but severely limited industrial growth on the island. See Norman Girvan, *Foreign Capital and Economic Underdevelopment in Jamaica* (Mona, Jamaica: Institute of Social & Economic Research, 1972); Iserdo Jainarian, *Trade and Underdevelopment: A Beyond the Badman Mystique Study of the Small Caribbean Countries and Large Multinational Corporations* (Georgetown, Guyana: Institute of Development Studies, 1976).

10. *Statistical Yearbook of Jamaica 1990* (Kingston: Statistical Institute of Jamaica).
11. Official rates of unemployment, even for economies with "advanced" methods for estimating number of unemployed persons, are always suspect. That is why instead of focussing on unemployment rates *per se*, I choose to present a comprehensive analysis of the island's labour force situation. But for whatever it's worth, official annual unemployment rates in Jamaica for most of the years since independence have ranged from a low 15 percent to a high of 30 percent. Most experts believe that in late 1980s and beyond, the real unemployment rate, exclusive of any calculation for underemployment, stood at well above 50 percent for youths sixteen to twenty-five years old.
12. See Errol Miller, "Educational Development in Independent Jamaica," in Rex Nettleford (ed.), *Jamaica in Independence* (Kingston, Jamaica: Heinemann Caribbean, 1989), pp. 205–227.
13. See "Going Foreign," a special *NACLA Report on the Americas* XV (January–February 1981).
14. U.S. Department of Commerce, Bureau of the Census, *Statistical Abstract of the United States 1992* (Washington, D.C.: U.S. Government Printing Office).
15. *Ibid.*
16. "Going Foreign," *op. cit.*
17. Most helpful to this discussion were the late George Beckford's penetrating analyses of the Jamaican plantation economy and the rise of the Jamaican peasantry. See, e.g., George L. Beckford, *Persistent Poverty* (New York: Oxford University Press, 1972); ——— and Michael Witter, *Small Garden . . . Bitter Weed* (Morant Bay, Jamaica: Maroon Publishing House). See also Catherine A. Sunshine, *The Caribbean* (Washington, D.C.: Ecumenical Program on Central America and the Caribbean [EPICA], 1980).
18. See W.F. Maunder, *Employment in an Underdeveloped Area: A Sample Survey of Kingston, Jamaica* (New Haven: Yale, 1960).
19. Ken Post, *Arise Ye Starvelings: The Jamaican Labour Rebellion of 1938 and Its Aftermath* (The Hague: Martinus Nijhoff, 1978).
20. Maunder, *op. cit.*
21. W.A. Blake, *Notes on Discussion on West Kingston Slums* (Kingston, Jamaica: Farquerharson Institute of Public Affairs, 1965).
22. Stuart Hall, "The Politics of Mugging," in Stuart Hall, et. al. (eds.), *Policing the Crisis* (London: Holmes & Meier, 1978), p. 375.
23. Richard Quinney, "Crime and the Development of Capitalism," in Richard Quinney (ed.), *Capitalist Society* (Homewood, Il.: Dorsey, 1979), p. 330.

24. *Ibid.*
25. Terry Lacey, *op. cit.*, pp. 33–34.
26. *Ibid.*, p. 34.
27. See Horace Campbell, "Bob Marley—Reggae, Rasta and Resistance," *Caribbean Contact*, 9 (July 1981), pp. 12–13; Rex Nettleford, *Mirror Mirror* (Kingston, Jamaica: Collins and Sangster, 1970); Walter Rodney, *The Groundings With My Brothers* (London: Bogle-L'Overture, 1969).
28. In fairness, the song was more a reflection, a caricature even, of the violence of the times than an endorsement of it. In a way, many of these late-1960s through early-1980s reggae songs sometimes carried serious political messages. The opposite is true for much contemporary dancehall music, in which violence, including sexual violence against women, is its ethos.
29. Yvonne Satherswaite, "The Legal and Social Implications of the Suppression of Crime Act and the Gun Court Act," LL.B. dissertation (Mona, Jamaica: University of the West Indies, 1975). *Ganja* was introduced to Jamaica in the mid-nineteenth century by East Indian indentured labourers who were brought in to work on the sugar plantations. Since that time, folk and medicinal uses of the plant have been found among rural and urban working-class Jamaicans. In the 1930s, the Rastafarians made *ganja* a sacrament and ritualized its inhalation.
30. Faye V. Harrison, "Drug Trafficking in World Capitalism: A Perspective on Jamaican Posses in the U.S.," *Social Justice*, 16 (Winter 1989), p. 123.
31. *Ibid.*
32. "Gov't Said Suffering Setback in Bid to Control Ganja," *The Daily Gleaner* (August 14, 1984). In comparison, Columbia, regarded as the region's leading narcotics exporter, in that same year supplied, according to the *Gleaner*, between a "mere" 6,900 and 9,300 metric tons of marijuana to the United States.
33. In 1986, Jamaica's external debt stood at 3.3 billion U.S. dollars, making Jamaica the world's largest per capita debtor. See Bernard Headley, "Behind A Manley Victory in Jamaica," *Monthly Review*, 37 (No. 4, 1987), pp. 35–42.
34. Michael Thelwell, *op. cit.*
35. Carl Stone, *Democracy and Clientelism in Jamaica* (New Brunswick, N.J.: Transaction, 1983); idem, *Class, Race and Political Behaviour in Urban Jamaica* (Mona, Jamaica: ISER, University of the West Indies, 1973). See, also, Carlene J. Edie, *Democracy By Default* (Kingston, Jamaica: Ian Randle, 1991); Headley, "Structural Correlates of Dependent Capitalist Development . . .," *op. cit.*, pp. 197–204; Lacey, *op. cit.*; Evelyne Huber Stephens and John D. Stephens, *Democratic Socialism in Jamaica* (Princeton: Princeton University, 1986); "Jamaica: Roots of Electoral Violence," NACLA; *Report on the Americas* (Issue 14, 1980).
36. Michael Kaufman, *Jamaica Under Manley* (Westport: Lawrence Hill, 1985), p. 114.
37. Quoted in Doris Kitson, "Jamaica and the Electoral Coup of 1980," *Race and Class*, 29 (number 2, 1982), p. 173.
38. It could, of course, be argued that Mr. Manley having his picture taken with known gangsters need have no more nefarious meaning than Mrs. Roslyn Carter, wife of former U.S. President Jimmy Carter, having hers taken, in 1977, at a Chicago Democratic Party fundraiser with one John Wayne Gacey,

one of America's foremost serial killers. At the very moment when he was basking in the presence of Mrs. Carter, Gacey had stuffed away in the crawl space of his suburban Chicago house the murdered bodies of several young men and boys, whom he had reportedly raped and strangled. Was a fleeting flash photograph of Mrs. Carter with Gacey proof positive that she knew him beforehand and may have even had knowledge of his crimes? The mere suggestion would be absurd. As far as appearances go, Mr. Manley was no more of a gang banger simply because he was photographed with gang bangers than was Mrs. Carter an accessory to serial murder because she was photographed with Gacey. Interestingly, though, despite the potentially libelous nature of the story, the PNP failed to bring suit against CNN, as Israel's General Ariel Sharon and U.S. (Army) General William Westmoreland had done, with some success, against *Time* magazine and CBS News, respectively, for allegedly making similar slanderous allegations against them.

39. The Suppression of Crime Act, passed in 1974, "empowered any police officer, army personnel . . . or any other auxiliary which the Minister [of Justice and National Security] wishes to create, to enter any premises or business place, or stop any vehicle or person merely on the suspicion that a criminal offence has been either committed or is to be committed." See Arthur Kitchin, "Is the Suppression of Crime Act Legal?" *The Daily Gleaner* (January 24, 1988), p. 18A. During the 1970s, more than one English-speaking Caribbean government resorted to hastily conceived "Suppression of Crime Acts" and dubiously declared "States of Emergency." Both measures gave governments virtually unlimited police-military powers to suppress the political opposition. See Cynthia Mahabir, *Crime and Nation-Building in the Caribbean* (Cambridge, Mass.: Schenkman, 1985).
40. "Jamaican Election Ends an Era," *The Washington Post* (March 31, 1993).
41. *Ibid.*
42. "Peril at the Gates . . .," an address by the Hon. Dennis Lalor at the *Gleaner* Honour Awards Banquet, April 5, 1992; quoted in *The Jamaican Weekly Gleaner*, North American Edition (April 16, 1993).
43. Stephens and Stephens, *op. cit.*, p. 237.
44. A number of prominent politicians have been known to use their power to physically remove a "top ranking" who turns out to be a source of political discomfiture. By relocating a disgruntled henchman overseas, a political benefactor is assured silence on potentially damaging matters. One police confidant told me he has seen ("with his own two eyes") leading politicians of *both* the JLP and PNP personally escorting known gunmen onto aircraft bound for "foreign." In fact, this officer (who for obvious reasons has to remain unnamed) said he was on more than one occasion "ordered" to conduct similar escorts.
45. Such was the case with Bob Marley. While still young, the future reggae star's mother had left him in Jamaica for work in Delaware, in the United States. She was able to send for the youngster while he was still a teenager. Marley, however, never liked America. He returned home after a short time.
46. See, e.g., Herman and Julia Siegel Schwendinger, *Adolescent Subcultures and Delinquency* (New York: Praeger, 1985); William J. Wilson, *The Truly Disadvantaged* (Chicago: University of Chicago, 1987).

47. Implicitly aiding and abetting the process of linkage have been the strong generalized sense of community, a spirit of inseparability with the home country, and insistent cleaving to native lifestyles that exist among many overseas working-class Jamaicans.
48. George L. Beckford, *Persistent Poverty, op. cit.*

## *Chapter 3*

1. Steven F. Messner, "Economic Discrimination and Societal Homicide Rates: Further Information on the Cost of Inequality," *American Sociological Review,* 54 (August 1989), pp. 597–611.

## *Chapter 4*

1. The American experience with guns and firearms is fitting example; see Erik Larson, *op. cit.*
2. See "Human Rights in Jamaica . . .," *op. cit.*
3. See "Jamaica: The Death Penalty," Amnesty International (New York, February 1989).
4. United Nations, *Development, Human Rights and the Rule of Law* (New York: Pergamon, 1981).
5. Bernard Headley, 1982, *op. cit.*
6. See, e.g., Norman Girvan, *op. cit.*; Iserdo Jainarian, *op. cit.*
7. See David Barkin, *Distorted Development: Mexico in the World Economy,* (Boulder: Westview, 1990); Arthur MacEwan, "Banishing The Mexican Revolution," *Monthy Review,* 43 (November 1991), pp. 16–27.
8. MacEwan, *Ibid.*, p. 22.
9. See Derick A.C. Boyd, *Economic Management, Income Distribution, and Poverty in Jamaica* (New York: Praeger, 1988).
10. For a thorough discussion of the two concepts, see Michael Todaro, *Economic Development in the Third World* (New York: Longman, 1981).
11. Elliott Currie, *Confronting Crime* (New York: Pantheon, 1985), p. 169.
12. John Braithwaite and Valerie Braithwaite, "The Effect of Income Inequality and Social Democracy on Homicide," *British Journal of Criminology,* 20 (January 1980).
13. Steven F. Messner, "Income Inequality and Murder Rates: Some Cross-National Findings," *Comparative Social Research,* 3 (1980).
14. Judith R. Blau and Peter M. Blau, "The Cost of Inequality: Metropolitan Structure and Violent Crime," *American Sociological Review,* 47 (February 1982).
15. *Development, Human Rights and the Rule of Law, op. cit.*, p. 95.
16. *Ibid.*
17. Paulo Freire, *Pedagogy of the Oppressed* (New York: Herder and Herder, 1970).
18. *Jamaica Five-Year Development Plan 1990–1995* (Kingston: Planning Institute of Jamaica, 1990), p. 65.
19. *Ibid.*

20. The prescription to eliminate subsidies is one of a family of four World Bank–IMF remedies; the others are get government out of the economy (in other words, privatize), push exports, and discourage imports.
21. John A. Peeler, "Alarm Bell for Third-World Democracies," *The Christian Science Monitor* (March 13, 1992).
22. *Ibid.* p. 19.
23. *Ibid.*
24. Quoted in Carroll D. Wright, "Labor, Pauperism, and Crime," *Proceedings of the 5th Annual Conference of Charities* (Boston, 1878), pp. 154–155.
25. *Ibid.*, p. 161.
26. Annual Report 1990–1991, Kingston Restoration Company.
27. "Boston Youths Serve Community," *The Christian Science Monitor* (January 25, 1993).
28. "Program Helps Teens in Trouble," *The Christian Science Monitor* (April 1, 1993), p. 13.
29. "YouthBuild: New Start for Young Adults," *The Christian Science Monitor* (December 22, 1992), p. 12.
30. Dermot Hussey, "One Hundred Years Old and the Alpha Boys Band Plays on," *SkyWritings* (December 1992/January 1993), p. 43.
31. *Ibid.*
32. Flier, National Youth Camp–Jamaica.
33. See, e.g., Albert Cohen, *Delinquent Boys* (New York: Free Press, 1955).

## *Chapter 5*

1. The *Statistical Yearbook of Jamaica 1981* (Government of Jamaica, Department of Statistics) records an actual count of 943 homicides for 1980.
2. *Trends in Crime and Criminal Justice, 1970–1985, in the Socio-Economic Context of Change* (New York: United Nations, 1992); see also Jorge A. Montero, "Costa Rica," in Elmer H. Johnson (ed.), *International Handbook of Contemporary Developments in Criminology* (Westport, Conn.: Greenwood Press, 1983).
3. But, skeptics might charge, 1980 was a particularly high homicide year for Jamaica, given the volatility of the political situation. Further examination of the Costa Rican figures reveal, however, that during the 1970s, the period for which I was able to access comparable crime data, Costa Rica's homicide rate remained relatively stable at or near the five per 100,000 population figure whereas Jamaica's ranged between 17.0 and 22.0 per 100,000 (see chapter three).
4. In the 1993 edition of the United Nations' *Human Development Report*, which measures wealth as a quality of life in the nations of the world, Costa Ricans are rated as living longer, as "better off" and "better educated" than just about all their neighbours; they also "enjoy cleaner water and better sanitation." Costa Rica ranks among a small group of countries doing a good job, the report says, "translating their [national] income into the lives of their people." Cited in "New U.N. Index Measures Wealth as Quality of Life," *The New York Times* (May 23, 1993).
5. Robert Trojanowicz and Bonnie Bucqueroux, *Community Policing: A Contemporary Perspective* (Cincinnati: Anderson Publishing Co., 1991), p. xiii.

6. *Ibid.*, pp. xiii–xv.
7. See "Human Rights in Jamaica . . .," *op. cit.*
8. Quoted in Leon Radzinowicz and Joan King, *The Growth of Crime* (New York: Basic Books, 1977), pp. 199–200.
9. These and other similar results were compiled for the Illinois Task Force on Crime and Corrections and appear in its final report (State of Illinois, March 1993).
10. *Prison Conditions in Jamaica* (New York: Americas Watch, May 1990), p. 7.
11. *Ibid.*, p. 10.
12. See Norval Morris, "Punishment Without Prison," Chicago Tribune (March 20, 1992);——— and Michael Tonry, *Between Prison and Probation: Intermediate Punishments in a Rational Sentencing System* (New York: Oxford University Press, 1990).
13. Illinois Task Force, Final Report, *op. cit.*
14. *Ibid.*
15. Cited in Morris and Tonry, *op. cit.*
16. "Government Will Not Change its Position on Hanging, Says PM," *Jamaica News*, IV (No. 2, March 1993), p. 3.
17. *When the State Kills. . . .* (New York: Amnesty International, 1989), p. 1–2.
18. *Ibid.*, p. 155.
19. "Amnesty Int'l Concerned About Fairness of Reviewed Death Cases," *The Sunday Gleaner* (May 2, 1993).
20. Quoted in *When the State Kills . . .*, *op. cit.*, p. 3.
21. *Ibid.*, p. 5.
22. *Ibid.*
23. See, e.g., David Dolinko, "Supreme Court Review—Forward: How to Criticize the Death Penalty," *Journal of Criminal Law and Criminology*, 77 (1986), pp. 546–601.
24. Quoted in *When The State Kills . . .*, *op. cit.*, p. 6.
25. Quoted in *When The State Kills . . .*, *ibid.*, p. 14.

*Chapter 6*

1. Quoted in "Advocate for a Community Ethos," *The Christian Science Monitor* (April 19, 1993); see also his book, Amitai Etzioni, *The Spirit of Community: Rights, Responsibilities, and the Communitarian Agenda* (New York: Crown, 1993).

# Index


Agriculture
  employment in, 23
  re-emphasis on, 51–52
Amnesty Int'l, 82, 85
Anti-Crime Investigation
    Detachment (ACID), xix

Beckford, George, 39
Bustamante, Alexander, 26

Communitarian agenda, 91–92
Community policing, 67–70
Crime
  in U.S., xv–xvi, 8
  numbers, 6–10
  prevention, xviii–xix, 45–67
  rates, 5, 8–9
  root causes, 13–15, 18–19

Davidson, Winston, 73
Death penalty, 81–87
Drug-demand reduction, 73
Drug trafficking, 2–4, 10, 38

Economic discrimination, 41–42
Economic inequality, 46–47
  and crime, 48

Fraser committee, 83

Garvey, Marcus, 89
Girvan, Norman, xviii
Gun court, 34
  deaths, xv, xvi
  running, 34

Hall, Stuart, 29
Harrison, Faye, 31

Ideology, xvii
  of crime, xviii
Immigration, 25
International Monetary
    Fund (IMF), 52–54

Jamaica Council for Human
    Rights, 85
Jamaica Labour Party (JLP), xi, 32, 33,
    34, 36, 96

King, Coretta Scott, 87
King, Martin Luther, Jr., 20, 81
Kingston Restoration Company
    (KRC), 57

Lalor, Dennis, 34
Law enforcement, 66–71

MacMillan, Col. Trevor, 91
Manley, Michael, 33, 34, 95
Manley, Norman, 26
Marley, Bob, 103ff.
Maroons, 89
Micro Investment Development
    Agency (MIDA), 57
Military, 64
  and crime, 65–66

Nettleford, Rex, xii, 14
Nongovernmental Organizations
    (NGOs), 50, 52

O'Conner, Flo, 74
Operation Ardent, xi
Outmigration, 24, 25, 27

Patterson, P.J., xi, 82
Peace Treaty, 34

People's National Party (PNP), xi, 32, 34, 36, 46, 52, 55, 96
Political patronage, 32
Political victimization, 32
Political violence, 32–34
Posses, 3–4
Prison
  conditions, 77
  overcrowding, 76–77
  solutions to, 78–81
Privy Council, 84, 85

Rastafarianism, 64
Re-exportees, 38–39
Rhygin, 90
Rosemary Development Fund, 57

Seaga, Edward, xi, 31, 33, 95
Sharpe, Sam, 89
Stewart, Gordon "Butch," xi, xxi
Stone, Carl, 32, 91
Sugar estate, 22, 25–27
Suppression of Crime Act, 34

Top ranking, 32–35
Tosh, Peter, 5

United Nations (UN), 46, 49, 86
United States Agency for Int'l Development (USAID), 56

Wailer, Bunny, 50